PRAISE FOR *RETHINKING REPUTATION*

"The authors are good storytellers, with tales of the famous and the obscure. They are especially good at conveying the power of character-based communication."

—Rudy Giuliani, former mayor of New York City

"Personal reputations seem in tatters everywhere you look today. This entertaining guide to public relations shows how the world's 'second oldest profession' is the basis of our individual reputations and relationships."

—Helen Ostrowski, retired chairman and
CEO, Porter Novelli

"Everyone knows that reputation is a bridge—and an illusion. *Rethinking Reputation* is a hands-on training book that drives away theoretic cobwebs and teaches you how to use modern PR to a variety of ends. You can give this book to your bosses, boards or other constituents to get buy-in for newthink strategies—while saving you from pulling out your hair!"

—Richard Laermer, CEO RLMpr and
author of Full Frontal PR

"In an age of public conversations, reputation maintenance is a daily practice, and your crisis management skills may be needed at any moment. Fraser Seitel and John Doorley's book *Rethinking Reputation* doesn't just shed light on PR best practices; it's a wake-up call and a must-read for all communications professionals today."

—Deirdre Breakenridge, CEO Pure Performance
Communications and author of
Social Media and Public Relations

RETHINKING REPUTATION

How PR Trumps Marketing and Advertising in the New Media World

FRASER P. SEITEL

JOHN DOORLEY

palgrave
macmillan

First published in 2012 by PALGRAVE MACMILLAN® in the United States—
a division of St. Martin's Press LLC, 175 Fifth Avenue, New York, NY 10010.

Where this book is distributed in the UK, Europe and the rest of the world, this
is by Palgrave Macmillan, a division of Macmillan Publishers Limited, registered
in England, company number 785998, of Houndmills, Basingstoke, Hampshire
RG21 6XS.

Palgrave Macmillan is the global academic imprint of the above companies and
has companies and representatives throughout the world.

Palgrave® and Macmillan® are registered trademarks in the United States, the
United Kingdom, Europe and other countries.

ISBN: 978-0-230-33833-3

Library of Congress Cataloging-in-Publication Data

Seitel, Fraser P.
   Rethinking reputation : how PR trumps marketing and advertising in the
new media world / Fraser P. Seitel, John Doorley.
      p.   cm.
   Includes bibliographical references.
   ISBN 978-0-230-33833-3
   1. Public relations. 2. Publicity. 3. Internet in public relations. 4. Internet in
publicity. 5. Reputation. 6. Corporate image. 7. Social media. I. Doorley, John.
II. Title.
HD59.S365   2012
659.2—dc23

                                                                    2012011583

A catalogue record of the book is available from the British Library.

Design by Letra Libre Inc.

First edition: August 2012

10   9   8   7   6   5   4   3   2   1

Printed in the United States of America.

CONTENTS

ACKNOWLEDGMENTS

WE WOULD LIKE TO THANK, FIRST, THE VARIOUS INDIVIDUALS, BOTH friend and foe alike, whose reputations we cite in this book. Without their stories, there would have been no *Rethinking Reputation*.

There are several others we would single out for special mention.

- First, our punctilious Palgrave Macmillan editor Emily Carleton, who did a valiant job enhancing our prose while keeping it grammatical and intact.
- Second, our illustrious literary agent Andrew Wylie, who the *Wall Street Journal* properly identified as the "superagent . . . who stands foursquare for literary elitism and good old-fashioned standards." We do hope this book hasn't lowered those standards appreciably.
- We would also like to recognize Ernie Grigg, a young public relations practitioner and scholar who is a graduate of the New York University program we both teach in, the MS Degree in Public Relations and Corporate Communication. His work as researcher, proofreader, organizer and editorial manager was invaluable.
- Many thanks to another graduate of the NYU program, future PR star Aubrey Gooden, who introduced us to T. Boone Pickens, subject of chapter 4. Aubrey helped us with research and drafting that chapter. Mr. Pickens and his head

of public affairs, Jay Rosser, were both kind and considerate, and we're most appreciative.

- We also want to thank Aly Rowe, another star graduate of our NYU program, for arranging our introduction to the two young women entrepreneurs featured in chapter 1 and for her research and drafting assistance.
- We are equally grateful to our NYU grad Nadia Mostafa for her research assistance with chapter 3.
- Ray Jordan, chief communication officer at Johnson & Johnson, has demonstrated great grace under fire, as has his legendary company. Both Fraser and John teach in J&J's Academy for Communication Excellence & Leadership (ACCEL). Ray trusted us to tell fairly the story of the company's toughest reputational challenge ever and we are grateful for that.
- Autobiographies of P. Roy Vagelos and T. Boone Pickens were most helpful in our research for chapters 3 and 4 respectively: *Medicine, Science and Merck* by Roy Vagelos and Louis Galambos; and *The First Billion Is the Hardest* by T. Boone Pickens.

Finally, John thanks his wife, Carole, his son, Jonathan, his daughter, Nanci, and all family and friends for their love and support. Fraser, too, thanks John's wife and family, as he doesn't quite understand how such wonderful people can tolerate such a needy individual. Thank you all.

THE AUTHORS

FRASER P. SEITEL IS A PUBLIC RELATIONS CONSULTANT, AUTHOR, teacher, lecturer, columnist and media commentator, appearing frequently on the Fox News network and other outlets. CNN's Larry King called Seitel "the man who practically wrote the book on PR." The 11th edition of Seitel's book *The Practice of Public Relations*, used at 200 US colleges and universities as well as at universities worldwide, was published by Prentice Hall/Pearson in 2010. The book's foreword was written by prominent banker and philanthropist David Rockefeller, with whom Seitel has worked for four decades. In his writings and comments, Seitel is an outspoken defender of and advocate for the practice of public relations as an "honest broker" between management and its publics. As he told National Public Radio's *On the Media* in 2007, "The cardinal rule of public relations is to never lie."

John Doorley is founding academic director of the Master of Science Degree Program in Public Relations and Corporate Communication at New York University's School of Continuing and Professional Studies. It is the world's largest graduate program in the field and the one named America's Best Public Relations Education Program in 2009 and 2010. Previously, until 2000, he was head of corporate communication at Merck & Co., Inc., which was named America's Most Admired Company for seven of his twelve years there (annual *Fortune* magazine survey). He has been the chief speechwriter for CEOs of major firms, has co-authored one of the most successful texts on reputation *(Reputation Management),* and has copyrighted a process to help firms measure, analyze, monitor and manage their reputations. He developed and taught the world's first undergraduate course in reputation management, at Rutgers University in 2002, and the first such graduate course, at NYU in 2012.

"Character is like a tree and reputation like its shadow. The shadow is what we think of it; the tree is the real thing."

—Abraham Lincoln

IT ALL STARTED WITH MOSES

Reputation rĕp ū tā tion (noun)

1. The sum of perceptions that individuals or groups have of a specific individual or organization.
2. A function of performance, behavior, communication and identity (what the individual or organization stands for).
3. The reflection of one's character.
4. What others think of you.

Public Relations pŭb lĭc rē lā tions (noun)

1. The art of communicating on behalf of an individual, company or other organization, mainly through unpaid channels ("earned media") and often with the goal of gaining third-party support.
2. The art of managing communication and relationships.
3. The poor man's alternative to advertising. The smart man's alternative to advertising.
4. The best communication strategy for managing reputation.

PUBLIC RELATIONS IS ONE OF THE MOST POWERFUL FORCES IN modern society. Neither marketing nor its subset, advertising, can deliver what public relations can for the large organization, the small one or the individual. It used to be that marketing and advertising were king, with public relations the vassal. Now, total expenditures for PR and word of mouth in the United States and other countries are increasing while total expenditures for advertising are steadily decreasing. And public relations is, let's face it, a heck of a lot cheaper. In more and more companies today, essentially for the first time, marketing reports to public relations.

That is not to say that marketing and advertising are not important in reputation management. In fact, the best communication campaigns, by large or small organizations, or by individuals, often incorporate public relations, marketing and advertising. What we are saying is: public relations trumps marketing and advertising.

Public relations has made many people rich. It has elected presidents and prime ministers and created mega-million-dollar success for plenty of individuals and businesses that could not afford advertising. It has helped convince millions of people to support ideas they first thought off-putting, or even contrary to their beliefs, has rallied millions to war and has even been responsible for the birth— and death—of nations. Think Arab Spring!

PR also has ruined people and organizations. Its misapplication has turned victory into defeat, success into failure and stardom into ignominy for countless politicians, celebrities, athletes and once high-flying CEOs and companies, all of whom have paid the price for their arrogance, hubris and failure to recognize the will of the people.

In the 1956 movie *The Man in the Gray Flannel Suit*, Tom Rath, played by Gregory Peck, returns a hero from World War II to a job that does not pay enough. A friend suggests a job in public relations, but Peck demurs: "But I don't know anything about public relations." The friend replies, "What do you need to know? You got a clean shirt, and you bathe every day. That's all there is to it."

And back then, it was often true. More often than not, PR was fluff, eyewash, meaningless hyperbole. Today, the public relations profession is thriving. There are 320,000 PR professionals in the United States and about 700,000 in Europe. The US government alone employs tens of thousands of PR professionals, including some 7,000 at the Pentagon. The president of the United States considers his spokesperson among his closest counselors. PR has become a validated social science, with hundreds of universities offering undergraduate and graduate degrees in public relations. All over the world, PR practice and study are booming.

The twenty-first century promises to be the Golden Age of Public Relations. Today, more and more, PR is replacing advertising as the go-to promotional strategy for individuals and organizations throughout the world. In more and more corporations, including the mammoth IBM, the marketing and advertising departments now report to public relations; not long ago, it was the other way around. In fact, in most companies today, public relations encompasses a wide swath of promotional and reputation management functions—media relations, employee communication, executive communication or speechwriting, corporate social responsibility, lobbying, crisis communication, shareholder communication, issues management and social media with its free-for-all blogosphere.

In this book, we tell stories of how people successfully used PR to accomplish remarkable things—or, just as often, immolated themselves, often needlessly. Most of these stories are contemporary, some focusing on the famous and others on the obscure. All have crucial lessons to offer.

PR itself is an ancient art form. It ain't rocket science, but it has a grounding theory and a long history that folks today, no matter what they want to accomplish, ignore at their peril.

It all started with Moses. Born about 1,200 years before Christ, he was raised as one of Egypt's royal family, with all the trappings and privileges. But it turned out that he had been adopted as an infant by the pharaoh's daughter, who had come upon him after his mother had placed him in a basket among the reeds at the edge of the river. And it also turned out that he was a Hebrew, a member of one of Egypt's enslaved races. Though the pharaoh and his daughter had discovered that, they embraced him as one of their own, so he clearly had a sweet life ahead of him. Until, that is, he decided on what the neighbors at the time thought a very dumb career move—he came to the defense of a Hebrew slave being assaulted by an Egyptian.

Moses was a reluctant hero. Yet he gave up all he had to flee his home, become an outcast shepherd and wander the desert. And then, one day, God appeared to him in a burning bush and commanded him to free the Hebrew slaves and then unite their 12 tribes. To accomplish those things, he would have to become the Hebrews' commander as well as their community organizer and legislator.

But Moses had a big problem: he was a stammerer (thus the expression "slow as Moses") and therefore not a confident communicator. This speech impediment was a serious obstacle for the man entrusted with the Ten Commandments, history's first values statement, which had to be promoted to the people. And Moses was smart enough, like King George VI of the United Kingdom three millennia later, to realize that great leadership requires great speech. So Moses turned to his more loquacious and personable older brother, Aaron, to be his—and, by extension, God's (not to mention history's) first—*nabi*, or spokesperson.

Aaron was raised differently from Moses. When his brother was off receiving formal education at the royal court of Egypt, Aaron was back in the rural tribal land of Goshen, mixing with the common folk. Aaron gained a reputation for eloquence and persuasiveness. He was a natural to speak to the people and to deal with the Egyptian royal court, both on behalf of his brother. As such, Aaron became history's first public relations representative. And Moses became the first great leader in history to see the potential value and wisdom of retaining a professional communicator to help achieve important goals.

Thus was born the modern-day practice of public relations.

About 800 years after Moses came Aristotle, who by then had a lot of PR history to draw on. To this day, he remains one of the best communicators ever. Pupil of Plato and mentor to Alexander the Great, Aristotle was also, not coincidentally, the father of *rhetoric,* the art of persuasion through the use of written or spoken language. He believed strongly in promoting the social good (the equivalent of today's *corporate social responsibility*). He recruited highly literate Greeks, dubbed "rhetors," or rhetoricians, to travel throughout Athens persuading the people that to work for the good of the city-state was in their own best interest. He divided persuasive appeals into three categories, a taxonomy that is even more useful today: first, *ethos,* appeal through a spokesperson who is highly ethical or credible; second, *pathos,* appeal through emotion; and third, *logos,* appeal through logic, which was Aristotle's favorite approach. PR professionals and anyone looking to PR for a career boost will be well served by knowledge of how Aristotle reasoned and acted to promote his ideas and philosophies. Aristotle was not shy about promoting himself and, of course, he had the substance to back it up.

Some 300 years later came along history's greatest public relations practitioner, Jesus, the prophet whom billions have believed to be the Son of God, a figure so influential in history that he actually split it in two.

Of course the miracles did not hurt, but whether you're Christian, Jewish, Muslim, Hindu, agnostic or atheist, the influence Jesus had as persuader, as rhetor, as crusader, cannot be denied. No one in history, before or since, could match his skill as a storyteller, a critical skill for public relations practitioners. In building his church Jesus staunchly followed certain principles, including attentiveness to others, empathy, authenticity and a clear definition of success—in PR jargon, the objective. If you just "love thy neighbor," he said, then you will be happy. Now that's irrefutable PR advice!

While wondrous things have been done in the name of God, horrible things have been perpetrated as well. In the Middle Ages, perfectly honed arguments, based on ethos, pathos and logos, were used to rally millions of Christians and Muslims to wars that lasted about 200 years and cost millions of lives. The Crusades, in fact, are a prime example of wartime public relations, propaganda that persuaded men to battle when they really had no idea whom or why they were fighting. Such is the approach today of Islamic extremists who incite terror against the West. In fact, many of today's public relations challenges are the same as they were in the Middle Ages— most notably, how to fight blind hatred through communication and education.

Words have always been the coin of the realm in public rela- tions. (Indeed, a company's PR person is often referred to as "the wordsmith.") So it comes as no surprise that one of the best PR pros ever was William Shakespeare himself, who accomplished one of the most remarkable feats ever in entertainment public relations, with the unwitting help of King James I (of England, not Cleveland or Miami). The crowning of the first Scottish king of England in 1603 inspired the bard's famous tragedy *Macbeth*. While the play is theo- retically nonfiction, Shakespeare manipulated several details to flat- ter and entertain the new king and invited the king to attend its first performance. (We're guessing he did not have to pay.) Not only did King James enjoy the play, he made Shakespeare's group the preferred theater company of the crown, requiring several royal productions a year. What the king liked, the people liked, so Shakespeare almost instantly became a box office superstar. By using his talents to target an influential audience, Shakespeare enjoyed wealth and prosperity, paving the way for today's $1,000-per-hour image consultants.

The American Revolution is perhaps the greatest example of Aristotelean appeals: through emotion ("Give me liberty or give me death"); ethical persuasion (the leaders, from Washington to Jefferson to Adams, were seen as highly ethical and credible); and logic ("no taxation without representation" and Thomas Paine's *Common Sense*). Indeed, those founders were classically educated and often quoted Aristotle. They motivated the colonists to fight for independence at all costs. PR tactics included pamphleteering, public speaking and lots of media relations.

And not to put too fine a point on it, but in a very real sense, it was poor media relations that killed Alexander Hamilton (as well as, of course, a very lethal bullet!). The founding father and first US secretary of the treasury made mistakes in the press, including calling the sitting vice president of the United States, Aaron Burr, "despicable." Burr objected to the media mauling and challenged Hamilton to the duel that ended their differences (not to mention Hamilton).

Two founders of modern-day public relations, Ivy Lee and Edward L. Bernays, gained prominence in part because of their communication initiatives in support of the Allied efforts in both world wars. Like all family trees, that of public relations has many things to be proud of and many we would rather hide in the attic. Both Lee and Bernays exploited their war-time accomplishments to advance their own careers as well as the profession. To their credit, they saw public relations as a two-way process that works best when it is used to benefit both parties.

Both men were extolled: Lee by John D. Rockefeller, Jr. for rescuing the Rockefeller family from rebuke after a horrible massacre at an iron mine they owned; and Bernays by industrialists and sociologists for incorporating the principles of psychology in the practice of public relations. It was not unimportant that Bernays, whom *Life* magazine recognized as one of the "20th Century's Most Influential Citizens," was the nephew of Sigmund Freud.

Both men were excoriated: Lee for his involvement in a communication project that aided the Nazis; and Bernays for using public relations to help convince women to smoke in public. Nonetheless, the point they both stressed was that public relations can produce tremendous support for individuals, organizations and ideas, and that PR works best when enlisted for a good cause. As Harold Burson, founder of one of today's largest public relations agencies, says, "Public relations is doing good and getting caught."

In the twenty-first century, virtually every sector of society is touched on a daily basis by positive or negative PR: *business,* from the mystique of a seemingly irreplaceable CEO of Apple Computers, to the public relations lapses of the world's greatest investment bank, Goldman Sachs; *politics,* from an embattled American president retooling his image to combat charges of inadequate management of the nation, to an Italian prime minister who set a world record for the number of sexual misadventures under litigation; *sports,* from a basketball superstar condemned for staging a publicity-stunt coronation while turning his back on his hometown, to the destruction of household-name baseball stars who lied about steroids; *show business,* from the perpetual problems of troubled Hollywood starlets to the one-woman merchandise/media communication conglomerate known as Lady Gaga; and even *international relations,* from the social media–led overthrow of long-term Middle East autocrats, to the rapid fall and narrow escape from the slammer of the powerful head of the International Monetary Fund.

Let's face it, if many of the famous, eccentric authors of the past were alive today (think Goethe, Hugo, Hemingway or the Brontë sisters) they would be on Letterman and Leno and Conan, contacting their friends on Facebook and tweeting their followers. If they didn't, few would buy their novels.

At its best, public relations works to develop relationships for mutual benefit. It's that simple. And when PR works well, it has greater credibility than advertising, whether it's street cred or the more formal kind measured by the big polling firms—because when someone else says something good about you, it's worth infinitely more than when you say something good about yourself.

To be sure, we can't build a long-lasting, positive reputation without good performance and behavior and a healthy dose of honest, persuasive communication. At the center of it all, day to day and over the long term, must be what the academics call identity, or what Lincoln called character—what one stands for. That is what the stories in this book are about.

PART I

HOW TO BUILD REPUTATION

ONE

THE POWER OF RELATIONSHIPS

The Magic Slippers and the Exterminator

THE TWO YOUNG WOMEN, HARDLY MORE THAN GIRLS, FOUND themselves promoting a new product before they had even finished the prototype, or crystallized the vision of it in their minds' eye. They had hit some snags in developing the actual product, but never in the idea, never in believing in or selling the idea. To them, the product was never just a pair of slippers. Their slippers would be stylish and sexy and utilitarian all at once. Their slippers would be magical. The women were still young enough to believe in that.

Susie Levitt and Katie Shea met in 2008 in their New York University dorm. They shared two important characteristics at the outset: entrepreneurial spirit and sore feet. Within a few meetings, they conceived of a pair of slippers that fashionable young women could wear when their high heels became unbearable. In just under a year, days after their NYU graduation, they had turned their idea into a product and obtained big-time publicity in major media, both traditional and social. And arriving almost simultaneously with the news coverage was the first batch of slippers—via China to Katie's parents' garage on Long Island, the business's temporary distribution center.

The publicity would produce not only hundreds of orders from individual women, but offers from retail stores to stock and promote the slippers. Within months, retail availability would expand from a few stores to hundreds, and then to nationwide chains like Bed Bath & Beyond, Dillard's and Neiman Marcus. And then, soon, to 25 other countries. And Susie and Katie were still barely 23.

But we're getting ahead of a good story: how youthful zeal combined with relationship building and publicity established a successful business. In record time, with no paid advertising.

NYU would not appear to be a nurturing place, even for two smart, tough young women. The largest private university in the United States, it receives more applications than any other—and it rejects more than any other. It is very tough to get in to and it can be even tougher to graduate from. Its students are in and of the most competitive city on Earth.

Enter freshmen Susie Levitt and Katie Shea in the fall of 2005. They had never met, nor would they for three more years.

They had a lot in common: both blond, petite, gifted and children of the suburbs, Connecticut and Long Island, respectively. And both were driven.

Susie, the youngest of four children, was a good student in high school and a star on the girls' soccer team. She didn't like being told what she could not do, "which may help explain why I was also on the wrestling team throughout high school." Fact is, she was much better than most of the best wrestlers, almost all boys, and she was named an All American both her junior and senior years. Her parents encouraged the children to be self-sufficient, and one of Susie's brothers became a successful software entrepreneur in his 20s.

Katie, the oldest of four children, was also a good student. She was outgoing and competitive. Like Susie's, her parents encouraged the children to be self-sufficient. Her parents and uncles were

entrepreneurs, always looking at possibilities for new business opportunities. In high school, Katie was involved in a small eBay business that sold factory seconds of women's clothing.

Katie: "My grades in high school were not as good as most of
the kids' who get into NYU. I think that my experience in that small
eBay business helped me get in."

When Susie and Katie were introduced their junior year by a
mutual friend, it was a desire to form a business that brought them
together. They had a good idea, but it was their ability to form relationships, trust in the strength of those relationships and execute
their ideas that made them successful.

They became friends right away.

"We both had this desire to form our own business," Katie remembers, "and we immediately saw kinship in that." Within weeks,
over a glass of wine in Katie's room, they thought they had hit on an
idea for something special.

The two seemed to arrive at the idea simultaneously—going
from complaining about the discomfort of high heels to acknowledging their affection for such shoes to realizing there had to be a
way of having both style and comfort. Shoes that attempted to do
both seemed to accomplish neither; they came out either unstylish
or not significantly more comfortable than regular heels. They realized that what they were looking for was not a hybrid, but a comple-
ment to the heel that was not a sneaker.

Katie: "It's hard to look and feel good in a nice outfit with sneakers, even when people realize you are just wearing them until you get
to work or home."

Susie's sorority sisters understood immediately. It was intuitive
for such young women of the city. So the sorority became the focus
group for new product research.

"They reinforced our belief," Susie says, "that the shoe had to be
flexible, foldable and yet sturdy enough to wear on city streets. It had
to be functional and sexy and affordable."

But Katie and Susie realized that the product would not be complete without very special packaging that would make it fashionable, even glamorous, to be seen carrying a second pair of shoes. So they designed the wrist pouch for the slippers to include an expandable bag that could hold the regular or high-heeled shoes. Carry the high heels in the pouch to work or the theater or school and, later, carry the slippers in the stylish bag. Manufacture the slippers, the pouch, expandable bag and packaging in bright colors. Make a fashion statement. Prevent a blister.

"We thought we had a good idea, but we were not exactly sure how to proceed," Susie says.

The first big problem was that the $10,000 they had scraped together was just enough to choose a manufacturer, experiment with various samples and produce a first batch of slippers. It was not enough for lawyers, marketing, advertising or other start-up costs.

"We had already come to realize that our excitement produced excitement in others and that others wanted to help," Susie says. "Whenever we would start thinking we simply did not have enough money for prototyping and patenting and production and publicity, someone would provide it as a favor, pro bono as they say. It was amazing. The thing that tied our business plan together—from idea to sales—would be relationship building."

Susie and Katie both held internships on Wall Street during their time at NYU. Over that first glass of wine, though, in their junior year and at the height of the Great Recession, they decided to reject investment banking and leap feet-first into slippers. Susie's father had recently died of cancer, and her mother supported her entrepreneurial spirit. Katie's parents, as entrepreneurs, understood.

Susie: "I don't think either of us ever second guessed what we were doing. We had this conviction."

But their internships in investment banking had taught them a lot, and in their senior year Katie and Susie entered a business plan competition at the NYU Stern School of Business. They worked together, planning for the start-up of a company that would market the slippers. They made it to the semifinal round of the competition and got to know some of the judges—one in particular, Bob Klein, the CEO of one of New York's largest extermination companies, based in downtown Manhattan.

Katie: "We kept bouncing ideas off Mr. Klein, even months after the competition ended. He must have thought us pests, excuse the pun. Who would have thought that the male CEO of an extermination company could have such great ideas about fashionable, functional footwear for women?"

They then learned of another business plan competition sponsored by the online broker Alibaba, which specializes in linking the right manufacturer with the right product. They had learned of Alibaba through an article in *Entrepreneur* magazine.

Susie: "The Alibaba competition had a first prize of $50,000, and we thought we had a shot at it."

This time they made it to the finals, winning $3,000.

By the winter of their senior year, while juggling term papers and exams, they decided to go for broke—"expecting we might get there fast," Susie says. Pushing ahead, they found a lawyer at NYU who would help them file for a patent at no charge; worked with the Entrepreneurial Center at NYU, asking for any help the Center could provide; and they explored several manufacturers through Alibaba. They worked with that manufacturer online to design a prototype.

After weeks of give and take, the shoe ended up being a kind of ballet slipper with two reinforced soles, one up front and the other in place of the heel, so that the new shoe could be worn indoors or out, on any surface. It was comfortable and sleek and folded into a small pouch containing the expandable bag, all of which could fit on the wrist or in a purse.

They chose a firm in Shanghai, China, to make the prototype they decided to market. (They were comfortable working online, creating virtual relationships, because they had grown up with such relationships.)

Early on, they got the idea to call the new shoes CitySlips, alliterative and evocative of the kind of style young fans of the TV series *Sex and the City* might like. Did it work? They did research with that demographic, their sorority, and the answer was a clear "yes."

On May 29, 2009, they received the first shipment of 1,000 pairs, at Katie's parents' garage on Long Island, and they were all set for an orderly launch. Three days later, an article featuring them and their slippers appeared in the New York *Daily News,* the nation's fifth-largest newspaper. The orders flooded in, and the two scrambled to meet them. They set up a PayPal account on their website. The serendipitous publicity meant that it was too late to build new relationships. So they desperately reached out to the relationships they had fostered for years, recruiting family, friends and NYU interns to help fill the orders. Susie and Katie worked 15-hour days for weeks into the summer.

LIGHTNING IN A BOTTLE

The publicity from the *Daily News* article was like lightning in a bottle.

"It became a joke with family and friends and classmates," says Katie. "'Let's skip the pleasantries,' my Mom would joke, 'and get to CitySlips.' Now that I look back on it, it makes sense that we would gain publicity for the shoes before we actually had any to sell."

That first article sparked orders from retail distributors. "Our plan called for us to have at least ten New York–area boutiques at launch," Katie says. But the publicity and response altered that minimalist market thinking.

Why not go for the big chains while at the same time cultivating small boutiques? So they devised a plan with a timeline for selling to both the boutiques and the chains. They contacted everyone they "knew who may know someone" and used the referrals to correspond with the chain headquarters online. By the end of 2009, Susie and Katie had signed 300 retailers. But that was just for starters: on February 1, 2010, they signed the Dillard's chain, which has 300 stores; in August, they launched at Neiman Marcus, with its 42 high-end stores; and on November 15, they launched at Bed Bath & Beyond, with its 1,800 stores. By December 2010 they also had agreements with over 1,000 boutiques.

The total number of stores stocking CitySlips at the end of 2010, 18 months after the first batch was produced: more than 3,100 in the United States alone. By now the shoe was also being sold in 25 other countries, from Canada to South Africa.

"We still did not want to spend on marketing and advertising," Susie says. So they again turned to friends and acquaintances, who suggested they market via the shopping networks such as QVC and HSN. They viewed the shopping networks more as wholesalers and distributors than marketers. The shopping networks take a percentage of sales, so Susie and Katie did not have to pay the networks to promote their product as one normally would.

Susie: "If we had to do that, there would have been no shopping networks for us."

The young women turned out to be good publicists. During the summer of 2009 and into 2010 they wangled appearances on a couple of the major shopping networks in the United States and Canada. They appeared at trade shows before hundreds of thousands of women, which cost only their time.

From friends of Katie's aunt's cousin (seriously) they learned of a monthly shopping event for young and middle-aged women called Shecky's Girls' Night Out. Vendors display their product lines, as they might have Tupperware in the 1960s and '70s, at a rented venue such as a nightclub. The shoppers get a drink or two or more and, usually, buy something.

Susie: "That experience gave new meaning to the relationship principle 'Six Degrees of Separation.' In our experience so far, it takes just three or four to reach just about anybody."

Katie: "We had great fun at Shecky's two different times in late 2009. We sold some shoes, but the main advantage, we're sure, was in the relationships we made, and in the word-of-mouth promotions and endorsements."

In other words . . . public relations. Or, in this case, accidental public relations.

Susie: "I don't think that Katie and I even thought it through— that we would use mostly public relations, and very little marketing or advertising. All we knew was that we couldn't afford advertising, and that PR was relatively free and results in third-party endorsements."

The article in the *Daily News* on June 1, 2009, three days after the first shipment of shoes was received, was part of a centerfold feature on businesses started by college students. The inclusion of CitySlips in the article was the result of the relationship the two young women had built with Jeff Carr of the Berkeley Center for Entrepreneurship at NYU's Stern School. He was one of literally scores of NYU staff and faculty Katie and Susie visited time and time again during their junior and senior years.

"When I was approached by the reporter for the *Daily News*," Carr said, "I immediately thought of CitySlips. Katie and Susie make an indelible impression—simply because of their enthusiasm."

Katie: "We were learning PR on the fly. One thing we learned from the *Daily News* article is that PR begets more PR."

Within days, major coverage ensued in *New York* magazine, *Forbes* magazine and on several blogs. On August 21, CitySlips was featured on the CNN home page—with a link to the company website.

Susie: "Once again, we were learning about the power of relationships. The CNN listing came about because one of my sorority sisters at NYU just happened to be interning at CNN. And I guess that is another lesson we will not forget—that relationships do not have to be with senior, powerful people to produce great results."

Relationships had served Susie and Katie well every step of the way, and they soon realized the importance of building a relationship with their customers. Social media proved to be an ideal outlet for starting "the conversation." Concurrently with the launch of the CitySlips shoe, they worked proactively to build a presence on the Internet's major networking sites. They embraced four of the media: Facebook, Twitter, YouTube and blogs.

Funk-tional Enterprises—the name of their new company—launched its first Facebook account in April 2009, a month before the first batch of the product was produced. This was a so-called Group Page to recruit people to join the conversation about flexible, functional women's footwear. The Fan Page, to recruit people who simply like the CitySlips brand and want to talk with others about it, followed in February 2010. They added the so-called Personal Account to recruit "friends" for frequent and personal conversation (the way most people understand and use Facebook) in June 2010.

Each account shares the same basic information, updates and contact information, though the Fan Page has rich visual content via multiple photo albums. Visitors are engaged with links to media placements, new blog postings and the occasional website that Susie and Katie feel is worthy of promotion.

"We not only listen to our members, fans and friends," Susie says, "we often accept their suggestions. A lesson we learned early on from Facebook is that we should treat our customers as our bosses." Susie and Katie always try to use a personal voice in their

Facebook posts so that members, fans and friends feel they are visiting a friend's page instead of a company's.

By late 2010, their Facebook group account boasted 1,129 members, an impressive number for a young, small company. By then their Fan Page was also robust, with 1,098 "likes," and their personal account had 217 "friends."

Funk-tional's Twitter account, @cityslips, debuted in early January 2010 and, by year's end, had 409 followers and 226 tweets. Susie and Katie use it as another vehicle to build and maintain the brand's invaluable connection with their customers. By being present on Twitter, CitySlips is telling consumers they care enough about these relationships to be available where their clientele is hanging out online. The content is essentially redundant of their Facebook posts, focusing on the media placement links and blog post announcements.

Funk-tional created a second Twitter handle, @cityslipsluxe, in the fall of 2010 in anticipation of promoting a line of higher-quality shoes.

The brand makes an effort to actively and regularly engage the Twitter community, utilizing @ messages, direct links and questions posed to followers. Each account has product-highlighting thumbnail displays and custom Twitter "skin" to jazz up the page.

CitySlip's YouTube account, www.youtube.com/cityslips, was created in July 2010. Most of their videos feature Susie and Katie introducing the product and promoting media placements. One video is a glimpse of the brand's vision for their YouTube future. It features a taxicab driver, recorded at a stoplight on a Flip Video camera, stating that one of the top reasons he sees girls heading home early on a club night is that their feet are sore.

The young ladies integrated their Twitter and YouTube followings to run online giveaways. For instance, @cityslips tweeted, promoting the giveaway of ten pairs to women who share via YouTube the best story about the last time they desperately needed CitySlips and didn't have them handy—or the most exciting, outrageous or compelling situation where CitySlips came to their rescue. In doing so, Susie and Katie hope to build their Twitter following while simultaneously enhancing their YouTube account with poignant and engaging fan endorsements.

Funk-tional Footwear's blogging effort has been a two-pronged initiative, both to capitalize via blogosphere promotion and to disseminate original content via their own WordPress blog. Called *Funk-tional Femmes: Innovative. Intelligent. Irresistible,* it debuted in May 2010 and has served as an excellent vehicle for building a more personal relationship with the consumers. Susie and Katie realize that their story of being young entrepreneurial businesswomen is far more compelling and advantageous—and drives stronger sales—than traditional product advertisements.

"Bloggers exist to blog, to opine," Katie said, "and we try to give them something to blog about." It's good old-fashioned PR—via the Internet.

In addition to introducing the public to the girls behind the shoes, Susie and Katie wanted to promote other female entrepreneurs and inspire still others to pursue their business aspirations. Susie and Katie want to share with other women, via the blogosphere, the success they've enjoyed. The blog is poised to lead yet another relationship-building effort, promoting other female-created products through personal interviews with these fellow female entrepreneurs, product reviews and reader giveaways.

Giveaways via social media hold special relationship-building potential. Each giveaway has its own special requirements, like tweeting a favorite product feature, which expands the brand's exposure well beyond the blog readership. CitySlips' messaging will "go viral," getting disseminated to all these readers' online relationships for retweeting and reposting. Additionally, having to take this or similar action crystallizes the brand name in the mind of the otherwise casual reader, helping to lend future credibility when next the reader comes across the product.

So how many people, in its short lifetime, has CitySlips reached in print media, on television, radio or online? According to basic "advertising equivalency correlation"—which commonly measures the size of the PR coverage gained, its placement and what the equivalent amount of space or airtime, if paid for as advertising, would cost—the number of people exposed to CitySlips by the end of 2010 was 12.4 million in the United States alone. The advertising cost would have been in the hundreds of thousands of dollars.

As Susie and Katie gained retail distributors, they expanded and refined their product line. They now sell the original CitySlips shoe through the boutiques and Dillard's at the original price of $25 a pair. They developed a more inexpensive shoe, called AfterSoles, for Bed Bath & Beyond, which sells for $10. For Neiman Marcus they developed the CitySlips Luxe, which has the same foldable and packaging properties, but is more durable and luxurious. The CitySlips Luxe shoes sell for $58.

Just as the line of slippers has expanded, so too have their markets, outlets and targets. Projections called for the number of American retail outlets that sell the shoes to grow from 3,100 to more than 3,500 by the end of 2012, and the number of stores outside the United States to be in the thousands as well. Funk-tional Enterprises now promotes to teens, working girls and moms, the maternity population, women who travel, women who have demanding careers and housewives who go out only on the weekends—with a specific approach to each demographic. Their original demographic was the sorority type. Their new one: women 16 to 60.

Susie said they expect revenues to exceed "several million in 2012, and that could grow fast in subsequent years. It's not that we're that ambitious, but one of the things we learned at NYU was that businesses that just try to stay static usually do not survive."

AS THEY WRESTLE WITH EXPANDING INTO NEW PRODUCT AREAS, THE CITYSLIPS creators remain true to their founding philosophy: products that are functional, glamorous, low-cost and fun; products defined by simplicity—in merchandise, marketing, communication and relationships. Guilt-free shopping, in other words.

In May 2010 they visited China to get to know the supplier who had been producing their product. They met with their agent, who goes by the Western name Teresa, several times and held dinners with her and some of her managers in formal settings in restaurants. After the meetings, the young American entrepreneurs felt "at home and at ease" with their international, intercultural business partnership, a primarily cyber-relationship now made more human. Now, at least once a month, the young women make a point of dropping a note to Teresa just to ask how she and her family are doing.

Susie and Katie have been diligent from the beginning about choosing partners who "do business right," as Susie says—no child labor, good working conditions and all the certifications that are reflective of a socially responsible business.

They sum up their philosophy on relationship building enthusiastically, each chiming in with an almost musical cadence. They mention family and friends and schoolmates and teachers and business associates. They mention the NYU teachers, Jeff Carr of the Center for Entrepreneurship, the lawyer who wrote their patent application, Teresa, women from Shecky's, the *Daily News* reporter who started the CitySlips ball rolling and their advisor the exterminator. Reminiscing, Susie and Katie both circle back to the parents who taught them the value of relationships—something both women say one must understand before going into business. They add that it doesn't hurt to keep relationship files on everyone who seems interested, who has a good idea or who lends a hand.

Susie: "Katie and I have worked with two very close friends, Courtney Spritzer and Stephanie Abrams, to help with our social media promotions. I met Courtney while studying economics at NYU and Stephanie during a Shecky's Girls' Night Out event. Soon after, I introduced them to each other and they have become great friends and business partners. Their company is called Collective Media, LLC, which is a full-service digital marketing and public relations agency specializing in social PR."

As for their own relationship, Susie and Katie both mention just one word: trust. And they add that they still enjoy relaxing together over, you guessed it, a glass of wine. Sometimes it's "scary" when they realize they will soon be employing more and more people, and that families in both the United States and abroad will be relying on them.

"In hindsight," Katie says, "fostering relationships before you need them is the key."

LESSONS

1. People want to help—just ask.
2. Don't wait until your idea is perfectly executed—the perfect is the enemy of the good.
3. Research is imperative and inexpensive—both at the beginning and along the way.
4. Public relations is mandatory; advertising is optional.
5. Trust: don't worry too much about people stealing your idea—you need to promote it!
6. Persevere!
7. Execute. Many people have great ideas for new products, but "execution is the key," per Susie and Katie.

8. Social media is a gift to marketers. Accept it. But don't ignore the traditional media.
9. Take notes and keep names on anyone who seems interested in your idea or who might lend a helping hand.
10. Relationships are like magic slippers. Cherish them!

TWO

THE POWER OF PUBLICITY

Penicillin for the Soul:
The Best Publicity Story Ever Told

THE THING ABOUT SUCCESSFUL PUBLICISTS IS THAT THEY ALWAYS think they can get others to say good things about their client or product or service, and they wonder why anyone would spend money on advertising and marketing when publicity is a lot cheaper and more effective.

"Why the average person doesn't spend more time publicizing his company or product or idea puzzles the heck out of me," John Frazier says. "Having others say good things about your product is a lot better than saying them yourself in an ad."

And John Frazier can prove it.

In 2009, he directed the American leg of the "Best Job in the World" campaign to promote tourism to the Australian islands of the Great Barrier Reef. His job was to announce the opening of a salaried, six-figure job as caretaker of Hamilton Island, one of 600 islands of the reef. News of the job, named with only a touch of hyperbole, broke on the evening of January 12 in the United States and simultaneously at dawn on January 13 in Australia. Within days, thousands were applying—young and old, rich and poor—and millions were watching the evolving reality show. It became arguably the most successful tourism campaign in history, and one of the most successful public relations campaigns ever. The results over just the first two days: 1,100 TV stations covered it in the United States alone, including all the network morning shows; there was massive print coverage; and the website with the job information got so much traffic—over one million hits—that it crashed, requiring the addition of nine more servers. Within weeks, the website received traffic from every country in the world except Western Sahara. (Do they even have electricity there?)

But we get ahead of our story.

The New York–based public relations agency John Frazier works for, Quinn & Co., had been hired by Tourism Queensland to promote vacations to the Australian islands. How could the Quinn team get people in the United States and Canada to want to go to Australia rather than to American beaches or the Caribbean? That was the challenge. Why spend an extra 12 hours on a flight? Why spend $10,000 for a suntan? Isn't a beach a beach? A commodity?

"We had to distinguish our beach," John says. He needed what publicists call "the big idea," and John knew what it would be as soon as he learned of the project. Create a job, a real job, a job at once fantastic yet accessible to anyone.

The client, Tourism Queensland, knew too, and had already created the campaign. There had been only a few such campaigns; one inspiration was the search for the first Chief Beer Officer, a campaign John had conceived in 2006 for Four Points by Sheraton Hotels.

Shana Pereira of Tourism Queensland: "What a bonus it was to learn that it was John who had created the Chief Beer Officer campaign. The world is definitely getting smaller."

John Frazier: "Most big ideas have a kind of simplicity, and the folks at Tourism Queensland, along with their ad agency, Cummins Nitro, put together the Best Job campaign so it had just four parts: (1) create a new, first-of-a-kind job, one almost anyone would want; (2) launch a global search to fill it; (3) alert the media, traditional and new; and (4) let the media do the rest."

> *Publicity Principle #1: There's always a*
> *big idea. You just have to find it.*

Quinn & Co. placed the ad in the *Wall Street Journal,* alongside the ads for senior executives and CEOs. It, too, had simplicity, just 72 words:

THE BEST JOB IN THE WORLD
Island Caretaker
Islands of the Great Barrier Reef, Australia

Full-time, live-in position with flexible hours. AUD $150,000 for a six-month contract. Accommodation provided—luxury home on Hamilton Island, overlooking Australia's Great Barrier Reef. Responsibilities: Explore the islands and report back; clean the pool; feed the fish; collect the mail. Apply to Tourism Queensland at island reefjob.com. Anyone can apply. (Refer to the terms and conditions at islandreefjob.com.)

The ad ran just one time, on January 13, and it cost $3,000. And that was it for paid advertising.

The price of entry was a video of one minute or less. More than 34,000 videos were submitted, and the story evolved to include the people who wanted the job, the people who needed the job, the job itself—and the islands. In the end, the publicity gained for The Best Job and the Australian islands was worth $400 million in advertising-equivalent print coverage in the United States alone. Add in the TV and radio and social media coverage, and the value worldwide was multiple billions of dollars. The entire worldwide budget for this project was about $2 million—mainly for the website, receiving and reviewing the videos, a modicum of advertising, and payments to Quinn and agencies in a few other countries. The return was thousandfold, accomplished almost entirely through public relations.

Most of the video submissions ranged from "good to excellent," John says. One, from a Canadian woman who is a weather reporter on television, was "as professional as anything you've seen." She emerged as one of the 15 finalists in the online voting. Another finalist was Cali Lewis from Dallas, a technology reporter on social media with tens of thousands of followers of her podcast, GeekBrief .tv, and as many more on her Twitter page. John and team were rooting for her.

John Frazier: "When promoting something in America, the top feeder market for tourism to Australia, it would have helped to have an American."

In addition to the 15 finalists chosen by Tourism Queensland there would be one wild-card finalist chosen by online voting, who turned out to be a young woman from Taiwan. She received more votes than the other 15 finalists combined.

"I think she got everyone on Taiwan Island to vote for her," John says.

In the end, Ben Southall, a 30-something charity fundraiser from the United Kingdom, was awarded the Best Job in the World. His frenetic 60-second entry and ensuing performance at the finals on Hamilton Island sealed the deal. His exotic experiences traveling the world and his excellent communication skills served him well as he spent six months trying to see and blog about as many of the hundreds of islands as humanly possible. He was interviewed by media around the world. He even appeared on *Oprah* via Skype.

So publicity, the core of public relations, is as old as Moses (remember, he convinced the Hebrews to follow him through the desert for 40 years); P. T. Barnum (he built a global enterprise of tents where people would pay to see other people, animals and things they would never want in their towns or homes); and Hollywood ("I don't care what you say about me as long as you spell my name right"). Today, publicity is bigger than ever, so ambitious companies, large and small, and individuals recognize the vast potential. This is the Golden Age of Public Relations, despite the alchemy that sometimes pollutes the profession.

But the Best Job in the World campaign—"priceless! We had a tiger by the tail," John says.

This is the story of John Frazier and how he became so good at a task that he believes every person and organization can benefit from. "That is not to say it's easy," he says, "because you have to convince others to say good things about you or your product or idea. And that is a lot harder than just placing advertising."

Melissa Braverman, who managed the Best Job campaign reporting to John, had joined Quinn & Co. in 2004 after seven years as a journalist that included stints at FOX and WNBC-TV. "The 'Best Job' campaign was one of the most exciting and professionally gratifying things I have ever worked on," she says.

She left New York on January 12 for Hamilton Island with eight journalists from the United States and Canada. They knew they were going to Australia but didn't know the exact destination. They arrived on Hamilton Island and Melissa took them, she explains, to "this absolutely beautiful house where the person who gets the 'Best Job' will live for six months."

Melissa Braverman: "So here we are in this island paradise, this absolutely yummy house, and we break the story to them. Some of the journalists joked that they would apply for the job themselves. One from the group actually did! Who wouldn't like a job living in this stunning house, walking the island or just sunbathing? You would get paid over $100,000 ($150,000 Australian) for six months' work. All you would be required to do would be clean the pool, feed the fish and blog about your experiences."

What makes Melissa so good at public relations, John Frazier says, is her passion. "She's a dreamer, a romantic. She embraces a new idea, a new project, like a new romance."

And this was a dream that the masses could hold. You didn't have to be a great singer or dancer or athlete or poker player.

"All you had to do was apply for a job that you knew would make you happy," Melissa says.

In your heart, you could be 18 or 22 again, dreaming of the perfect job. For this particular job, you did not have to settle. And although it was for just six months, anyone could see the possibilities that winning a big contest like this would present. And if you believed that desire counts for something, you believed you had a chance.

Just three days before the contest was announced, on January 9, the Department of Labor announced that job losses in the United States had hit a 16-year high at the end of 2008, and there were similarly dire reports worldwide. What a time to announce a chance at something great. Something aspirational! Hope!

"I believe that the campaign would have been successful any time," Melissa says. "But the fact that the contest coincided with the worst of the Great Recession did not hurt."

John Frazier calls the campaign "penicillin for the soul. A lot of people were hurting and we gave them some hope. Melissa and I and our colleagues in Tourism Queensland felt good about that."

In the end, he says, he is a publicist, a professional communicator who believes in the power of the word, the power of pictures, of storytelling and of positive, persuasive communication. He figured this out in his early 20s in Louisiana in the 1970s when an opening for a job as a typist led to one as a junior publicist, and then to a bigger

PR job in New Orleans, and then on to the big time in New York City. Today, luckily for him, PR is even more central as a discipline: every influential person or organization has a PR pro—actors, athletes, government officials, writers, religious leaders, entrepreneurs.

Even the smallest businesses need publicity in the current market, John says. "Success today requires knowing how to sell your idea. There is so much competition for attention, if you do not know how to attract it and manage it—your idea, your product—you will just not be able to break through.

"With the 'Best Job' campaign, we did one heck of a job for our client, Tourism Queensland. In the end, Quinn & Co.'s reputation and my own will rest on what we do for the client. We were also able to bring some hope and happiness to a lot of people and that's a bonus. But we were not out to change the world."

When pressed, he will concede that PR can help change the world, as it did in 2001 when his client was South African Tourism. As the country was approaching the tenth anniversary of the end of apartheid, the government wanted to conduct a significant campaign to attract tourists to the country. They set aside a large budget, and John was a member of the team that planned the multifaceted campaign. Then came 9/11.

"We were far into the planning," he remembers, "and the unthinkable happened. It cast a pall on the entire travel industry. Previously, Africa was seen as dangerous. Suddenly, New York was seen as the dangerous destination—and we saw the potential for Cape Town, Johannesburg and other cities that no longer seemed so scary. So the South African government virtually eliminated its advertising budget. But it maintained its public relations budget, even while tourism was crashing worldwide. So we were able to move ahead with the PR portion of the plan."

The key tactic here was to work with the airlines to help them see the tourism potential. It's hard to get the airlines involved in a tourism campaign, John explains, because they don't generally see the benefit to individual airlines. Somehow, John and his colleagues convinced South African Airways to set aside 100 round-trip business-class tickets for journalists from America to travel to the country free—an investment of almost half a million dollars.

John Frazier: "We used each ticket as if it were gold, weighing the potential benefits of sending one journalist versus another. We leveraged every single bit of good news that came from the country for one year."

The journalists who went experienced firsthand the beauty of the country and the resounding narrative of freedom. The news and features they filed gave the campaign a third-party endorsement—something advertising cannot do.

By the end of 2002, arrivals in South Africa from the United States alone were up by almost 10 percent. And this was during tourism's darkest hour, when people—especially Americans—were afraid to travel. It helped that the captains of the cruise ships that had once sailed through the Suez Canal in the Middle East now thought that route too dangerous, so they sailed down the West Coast of Africa, with Cape Town as a port of call. It also didn't hurt that the 44 million people of South Africa were determined to show the world how far its newest democracy had come in just ten years.

"You have to believe in what you're selling," John says.

The president of South Africa believed that for every eight tourists, one permanent job would be created. Thousands of people are working in South Africa now thanks in part to John Frazier and his colleagues.

The purpose of publicity runs the gamut, but the big campaigns usually have big ideas behind them. In 2004, soon after joining Quinn & Co., John landed Manhattan's soon-to-be-renovated Algonquin Hotel as a client. He was charged with repositioning the old luxury boutique hotel, which had fallen into disrepair.

The management of the hotel, which was once home to many great writers and artists, from Dorothy Parker to Edna Ferber and William Faulkner, wanted it to once again be the place to see and be seen. It was where Lerner and Lowe had written *My Fair Lady,* the *New Yorker* magazine had been born and the careers of Harry Connick Jr., Diana Krall and Michael Feinstein had been launched. And so, while the hotel was closed for repairs, the Quinn team got to work on a publicity plan.

How could Quinn & Co. modernize one of the hotel industry's greatest reputations without losing the patina of its past?

The challenge was that the media do not usually care about a hotel renovation story, even when it is one of the oldest hotels in NYC. They needed—you guessed it—a "big idea" that would make the old Edwardian structure competitive with the Trumps and the Hyatts, as well as the luxury boutique hotels then beginning to spring up all over Manhattan.

"We needed something that would make the morning and evening news, not just the trade press," John says.

Quinn & Co.'s founder, Florence Quinn, always places the highest priority on finding the right big idea. This case would be no different. In a brainstorming session attended by Algonquin General Manager Anthony Melchiorri and John and his Quinn & Co. colleagues Carla Caccavale and Vanessa Amador, the team focused on bringing back the martini, a drink popularized in the heyday of the Algonquin Round Table. But what new twist to give it? A coconut martini? A chocolate martini? A martini served on ice? At that point, Carla quipped that she knew what kind of "ice" she'd want in her martini.

"We all looked at each other and knew the a-ha moment had arrived," says John. "We would create the world's most expensive cocktail, the $10,000 Martini on the Rock served over the 'ice' of a diamond ring."

Now they needed to actually sell one. But first, they had to find the right couple. It took just a matter of days, and on December 7, with journalists pretending to be customers, Joe Imperato proposed to Melissa Beck. Flashbulbs popped. Melissa said yes. The story made the front page of the *New York Daily News,* the city's largest paper, and it became big on TV and radio. Once the story went viral, Regis Philbin, David Letterman and Ellen DeGeneres made light of it, and many of the morning shows, national and regional, featured it.

Until the Best Job campaign, the $10,000 martini reigned as perhaps the most successful travel and tourism campaign of the new twenty-first century, following in the footsteps of the Virginia Is For Lovers and I Love New York campaigns. But those iconic destination campaigns had used mostly traditional media. Ironically, the stodgy old Algonquin had been one of the first to exploit the power of social media. Today, years later, the $10,000 martini is still featured on the Algonquin Hotel's website. And it has added to its roster of employees (Are you ready for this?) a Chief Cat Officer to care for the hotel cat, the tenth in the line that has been roaming the lobby since John Barrymore dubbed the first one Hamlet in 1932.

These kinds of campaigns risk being called frivolous and even unseemly, but they are clearly powerful. And the "oldest tricks," John says, are often still the best. To make news it is still good to offer "the first" of something, the "biggest," the "most expensive," the "best."

"I think it's encouraging that 'the best' is still important to people," John says. The Algonquin is not just the oldest hotel in New York City; many people—me included—think it is the best."

John F. Kennedy: "When I was growing up I had three wishes. I wanted to be a Lindbergh-type hero, learn Chinese and become a member of the Algonquin Round Table."

The best publicity stories, like the Best Job one, actually *become* the news, rather than a news feature. And they have, as the publicists say, "legs"—different iterations and evolutions, so that one story becomes many. In the case of Best Job, John Frazier and his colleagues precipitated news coverage around many events, mainly these six: the announcements of the contest for the Best Job, the 50 semifinalists, the 16 finalists, the winner; the winner's job for the six months on the island; and the post-job media tour.

John credits Patrice Tanaka—his boss from 1987 to 1990, and partner in Patrice Tanaka & Company from 1990 to 2003—with being among the first to create an actual job in order to make news. And one of her guiding principles in approaching any communication challenge is that it should have legs. "No one-offs," as Patrice puts it.

Publicity Principle #2: Choose a strategy or tactic that presents more than one possibility for news coverage.

Patrice's first job creation, in 1989 for her client Korbel Champagne, was a director of romance, a real job that paid a real salary at Korbel. Upon landing the Korbel account, Patrice uncovered research that revealed 93 percent of American consumers associate champagne with romance. That finding was intuitive, yet incredibly important in constructing the PR campaign.

"We decided to exploit that finding," she says. She placed an ad in the *Wall Street Journal* Job Mart section—"Wanted: Director of Romance"—which cost a few thousand dollars. That was essentially all the advertising that was necessary. The rest was vintage PR on behalf of a story with many aspects and iterations.

Korbel received more than 1,200 resumes, from bankers, lawyers and chief financial officers who, Patrice remembers, "yearned for a little romance in their lives." Two people held the director's job over the next four years. Actually, Patrice and her agency created Korbel's Department of Romance, Weddings and Entertaining—the three most frequent occasions for champagne.

"The job, the department, we created was a kind of Trojan horse," Patrice says, "to get the story past the gatekeepers of the press, who were reluctant to do stories on alcoholic beverages and more receptive to doing stories on romance. But the job, the department, was real, with real job duties, including publicizing Korbel Champagne on every romantic occasion from Valentine's Day to New Year's Eve." The formula was the one John Frazier and colleagues would follow 20 years later with the Best Job campaign: create a real job that people will want, alert the press and so on. . . . Each step, including the non-events, produced coverage: "Director of Romance position not filled yet." The campaign ran for four years, contributing to a 50 percent increase in sales of Korbel Champagne, and this during a period when the champagne category was down 12 percent. The story had "legs."

"Today," Patrice says, "whenever I pitch prospective clients, I like to tell them that PR is the Hamburger Helper of the marketing mix. We can help stretch your marketing dollars at a fraction of the cost of advertising."

So you are a publicist. You found the big idea (Publicity Principle #1) and it has legs (Principle #2). The next thing to do is execute. Take care of all the details that will lead to success: an increase in sales of Korbel Champagne, for instance, from 800,000 cases to 1.2 million cases annually. Could advertising have accomplished what the director of romance did?

Execute!

Publicity Principle #3: Plan and execute as if your life depended on it. Generals do.

"When the 'Best Job' news broke on January 12, 2009," John Frazier recalls, "I was very excited. Tactically, it was an international challenge. I was in New York holding down the fort, and Melissa

Braverman was on Hamilton Island with the journalists, having just arrived."

Weeks before the Best Job announcement, Melissa had contacted Verna Gates, a journalist with the Reuters news service, and given her the story under a promise that she would embargo it until announcement day. But when Reuters learned on January 12, 2007, that a blogger had reported the story early, she released it over the wire, 12 hours sooner than planned.

John Frazier: "All along, during the planning for 'Best Job,' we thought it was critical to break the news in a coordinated way with our colleagues in Australia and Europe. But we adjusted quickly, and other journalists quickly started reporting. On the first day, an Associated Press reporter interviewed the manager from Tourism Queensland in the UK. The AP released video of the interview, which included beautiful footage of Hamilton Island and it was picked up all over the world that first day."

Shana Pereira of Tourism Queensland is based in Los Angeles. She was there on January 12, 2009, when The Best Job in the World story broke.

The campaign was creative, and it was activated to fill a specific gap, she says. "All activity we do is to meet an objective, and in this case, the objective was to raise awareness for the Islands of the Great Barrier Reef."

In this case, Tourism Queensland's research showed that most potential tourists believed the islands of the Great Barrier Reef are uninhabited. Tourism Queensland chose Hamilton Island for the Best Job because there are some 3,000 people living on the island, many of them working in tourism. What better PR strategy than to make people want to live there?

"The first step is identifying the gap and committing to an objective to address it," Shana says, "then what message and medium will be most effective in inspiring the people you are trying to attract."

When PR folks talk about execution, they use military terminology—objectives, strategies and tactics. For a discipline that is thought of as soft, that anyone in a clean shirt with a personality to match can do, many of them can quote Carl von Clausewitz, the Prussian general who wrote *On War*.

So if someone asks you what your strategy is, you ask him what objective he is referring to. If he asks what your message is, you ask which audiences he is referring to. For it is axiomatic to PR pros that the strategies and messages should differ for different objectives and audiences, yet always be consistent.

"When you have a great story," John Frazier says, "you go from planning and being strategic to responding. It becomes frenetic, and you start going by instinct—does what the reporter is saying to you seem honest, can you trust him? You just get into the mode of working all out for your product, your client."

But the perfect is the enemy of the good. Bad things happen in publicity because its process, unlike advertising's, cannot be completely controlled. But that is why PR, when it works, is much more credible.

Publicity Principle #4: When life gives you lemons, turn them into lemonade.

The first thing that went wrong with the Best Job campaign was the breaking of the news embargo by Reuters.

"Although this was disappointing at the time," Melissa Braverman recalls, "it turned out great."

Soon after the Best Job contest was announced, copycat job contests began to appear. Fraudulent entries did as well, with one from a presumed Osama bin Laden. The director of tourism for Taiwan announced a contest for a job there, changing one word in the Best Job ad. He was fired.

One of the 16 finalists for the Best Job turned out to be a Russian porn star. After some embarrassing publicity worldwide, she was removed from the competition.

The worst things in life can be helpful in publicity campaigns. Unfortunate events always present opportunities for someone. In 2001, as the announcement day drew nearer for the South Africa tourism campaign, 9/11 happened. In 2010, as the announcement date for Best Job neared, the economy worsened, hitting its lowest point since the Great Depression.

"You need to be tenacious," John says, "and good at working under deadlines and intense pressure.

"The character of the publicist always shows through in the campaign. Honest publicists produce honest campaigns and the corollary is true. I think it's also true that, often, the PR professional who is hired to promote a particular product has something in common with that product."

Patrice Tanaka puts it this way: "Whenever I first meet with a client or think about a PR campaign for a particular product, I try to identify the essence of the brand and then create a campaign to bring that to life."

It's even better to challenge the company to describe the brand, what they think it is, versus the reputation, what others think of it. Some call that concept simply "brand"; others, like Patrice, call it "brand essence."

Publicity Principle #5: Identify the brand essence.

In 1989, when Patrice challenged the communication people at Korbel to identify the brand essence of their champagne, the descriptions became long and complex. Eventually, Patrice worked with them to settle on one word: romance. And that would be the identity they would embrace going forward—for the company and the champagne.

Creativity was always part of the Patrice identity, her brand. Over the years, her agency's campaigns became increasingly creative. In 2001, she and her staff conducted a campaign to promote the Dyson vacuum cleaner at New York's Fashion Week by having Russian models strut down the runway with them—topless.

"It was edgy and bold," Patrice recalls, "but it was not crude. I would never go for that. By the next morning, a photo of topless models pushing the Dyson DC07 vacuum was the shot sent around the world. The *New York Times* ran a piece depicting the scene in a simple line drawing. *Women's Wear Daily* put the photo on the cover. We got such great coverage from the event that we were able to get the vacuums included in the celebrity presenter gift baskets for the Emmy Awards, which took place during the same time frame as the launch."

The campaign had "legs" and went on for eight months, generating sales of the vacuum cleaner 160 percent above forecast. It became the market leader, and *Time* magazine named the Dyson DC07 the Best Invention of 2002.

Fast forward to the fall of 2011. Tourism to Japan was languishing because of the earthquake, the tsunami and the damage to the nuclear plant in Fukushima. Not to mention the strong yen. If you had a plane ticket to Japan, you couldn't give it away . . .

So that's exactly what the Japanese Tourism Agency decided to do. In October 2011, the agency announced that it planned to offer free airfare to 10,000 foreign travelers in 2012. After parliament approved the budget, the agency set up a website to accept requests. The rules were simple. Applicants explained what they hoped to get out of the trip. Once accepted, they had to publicize the trip on blogs and social media platforms so the world could see that Japan posed little danger to travelers.

Within a few days of the announcement, inquiries flooded tourism offices, embassies and even media outlets carrying the news. Japan had gotten the world's attention, and the JTA knew exactly how to capitalize on that. The agency clarified that accepted applications would have to include "new ideas" for experiencing Japan. The web publicity required that the lucky winners highlight interesting and unique vacation ideas along with the country's safety.

"Brilliant campaign," John Frazier says.

Doesn't he see a little of his South Africa campaign there?

"You know what they say about imitation and flattery," he says. "Besides, who knows who thought of what first? Creativity always has ancestors."

Brand essence! Passion!

Shana Pereira of Tourism Queensland says, "Did you know that the Great Barrier Reef can be seen from outer space? It is truly one of the wonders of the world."

"We are not out to change the world," John Frazier says. "We are getting paid to do what our client needs done. In my case, I get to go to the best destinations and stay in the best places. I dreamed such things growing up in Louisiana. Growing up in New York City, Melissa Braverman dreamed of working in Australia. We both realized our dreams.

"Come to think of it," John Frazier says, "I actually have the 'Best Job in the World.'"

LESSONS

1. Timing is everything.
2. Use all media, traditional and new.
3. An embargoed story given to a journalist in advance in return for a commitment to hold the story until release date remains a winning publicity strategy.
4. Publicity requires passion.
5. Publicity Principle #1: Find the "big idea."
6. Publicity Principle #2: Choose a strategy that presents many opportunities for coverage.

7. Publicity Principle #3: Plan and execute.
8. Publicity Principle #4: Make lemonade out of lemons.
9. Publicity Principle #5: Find your brand essence.
10. And what is Publicity Principle # 6? "That's easy," John Frazier says. "Have fun!"

THREE

THE POWER OF YOUR PERSONAL OR COMPANY BRAND

P. Roy Vagelos, Maverick—Lessons in Leadership and Communication

FROM UNREMARKABLE BEGINNINGS, P. ROY VAGELOS GREW UP TO become a great scientist, to head one of the most successful companies ever, and to oversee the development of more important new medicines than any company introduced before or since. Along the way, he became a great communicator through the sheer quality of his character.

Talk about your American dream: you couldn't make this one up!

He was raised in New Jersey, the son of Greek immigrants who went through some pretty rough times during the Great Depression. Early on, he was not a good student. But while working in his parents' diner, he began listening to chemists who worked at Merck, then a relatively unknown pharmaceutical company, talk shop over lunch. Perhaps it was those chemists who inspired the boy to start focusing on something other than sports. Perhaps it was Ms. Brokaw, his Rahway High School algebra teacher, who told him he was smart, very smart. Something clicked. The boy went on to graduate Phi Beta Kappa from the University of Pennsylvania, and then from Columbia University's College of Physicians and Surgeons, at the top of his class.

By then, 1954, Pindaros Roy Vagelos had become P. Roy Vagelos, or simply "Roy." He liked medicine and helping patients, one at a time, but there was always another sick person right behind the one he treated. Tenacity was one of his strong suits, but patience wasn't. He wanted more, so he became a research biochemist, with no PhD, just on-the-job training at the National Institutes of Health (NIH) in Maryland, the world's most prestigious biomedical research institution. Within a few years he became head of a research group there and then moved on to St. Louis to head the biochemistry department at Washington University. And then, as if to prove Ms. Brokaw right, he moved back to Rahway, New Jersey, as second in command in the Merck Research Laboratories, where the chemists he used to eavesdrop on had worked.

And then—just when you thought this Horatio Alger script had come full circle—he became head of the Merck Research Labs, and then chief executive officer and chairman of the board. By then, it was 1985 and he was 56. He was just getting started.

Under his leadership, Merck became not only "America's Most Admired Company" but one of the world's most admired as well. The company's reputation soared in the late 1980s and early '90s to the point where its worth (market capitalization) was in the top five of US companies (and the top ten in the world), even though its revenues were only 5 percent of those of another top-five company, General Motors. Merck became a takeover target, and Roy Vagelos thought that DuPont, a much larger firm but one with similar values and commitment to science, might prove to be a good acquirer. But by then the Merck reputation had become so good that its high market capitalization made the company too expensive to acquire. For years to come, the reputational capital of innovative Merck would continue to exceed that of much larger firms like GM that had lost their innovative edge.

Roy Vagelos helped make lots of money for Merck, its shareholders and its employees. But that's not all he did. When some of his scientists came to him and said they thought they could help defeat river blindness, one of history's most devastating diseases, he encouraged them to proceed—even though he knew the company could not make a profit on the medicine that would later be known as Mectizan and even though he had no idea how to distribute it to the millions of victims, mostly poor and living in the bush in sub-Saharan Africa or remote parts of Latin America. And when powerful government scientists from Washington, DC to Geneva scoffed at the drug as too good to be true, and when policymakers warned him not to commit to donating the drug to millions of people for decades to come, he did it anyway.

Today, it would be virtually impossible for Roy Vagelos to walk into any of thousands of villages in Africa or large swaths of Latin America and not see adults who are blind because they were born too soon for Mectizan but are raising children who will always be able to see.

Some members of the Merck board of directors first found out about the 1987 commitment "to donate Mectizan to treat river blindness anywhere it is needed for as long as necessary" from the press. No one screamed, for by then they knew their CEO.

"No shareholders complained," Vagelos remembers, "not one."

And when in 1989 he decided to transfer to China, for a nominal sum, manufacturing technology and rights to a vaccine to prevent hepatitis B infection in newborns, Merck supporters knew better than to argue. Today, in 2012, it would be unlikely for him to visit

China and see a newborn child who has not been vaccinated against hepatitis B. By 2014, it will be virtually impossible; by then, all 25 million children born annually will be vaccinated within their first 48 hours of life against the hepatitis B virus, which until now often caused liver cancer and death.

By the time he retired from Merck in 1994, the company had received more honors than perhaps any before it: America's Most Admired Company; The World's Most Admired Company; Most Admired for Working Women; Most Admired for Working Mothers; Most Admired for Asians, Blacks and Hispanics. And on and on! Roy Vagelos had been lionized by numerous organizations and even by the press. Merck employees believed in him. They trusted him.

He had to retire as CEO at 65 because of the board's policy, but he could have stayed on the board, which was customary. He refused: "It is not fair to a new CEO to have one's predecessor hanging around, second guessing him or her. I left Merck, but I never retired."

Within months he became chairman of the board of directors of the young biotech firm Regeneron, because, as he said, "It is one of the few start-ups that has the right stuff to succeed." Sixteen years later, on November 18, 2011, as the result of much tenacity and some patience, Regeneron gained approval to market Eylea, its first significant new medicine, for the treatment of wet age-related macular degeneration, a common cause of blindness in people over 60. Roy Vagelos began that day with a three-mile run, knowing that Eylea "is going to help a lot of people." A few weeks earlier he had celebrated his 82nd birthday with Diana, his wife of 57 years, their four children and their nine grandchildren.

Between the time he left Merck and Regeneron's introduction of Eylea, Vagelos served as chairman of the board of trustees of the University of Pennsylvania, where he worked to enhance the chemistry program that he and his wife then endowed. He also served as co-chairman of the board of trustees of the New Jersey Performing

Arts Center and was a charter member of several initiatives to advance science education.

Roy Vagelos: "You cannot accomplish anything without being able to motivate people above you, below you and on the side. Over the long term, you can only do that by the force of who you are and what you stand for."

Academicians in communication call that one's "personal brand"—how one wants to be perceived—versus how one actually *is* perceived, which is called reputation. Ideally, the two should match. An individual's "brand," like a company's brand, distinguishes that person or organization from the rest. The company or the individual with a powerful brand is not a generic, a commodity. The brand says that everyone knows what to expect from this particular company or individual. The brand is a promise.

The Vagelos brand comprises leadership in business, new drug discovery and development, and worldwide community and corporate citizenship that have directly benefited millions. But Vagelos is also an educator, patron of the arts, avid athlete and, says wife Diana, "a terrific family man and partner."

His first appearance as a celebrity CEO was in a white lab jacket on the cover of *BusinessWeek* on October 18, 1987. The headline was just three words: "The Miracle Company." The writer, John Byrne, who later became the top editor at *BusinessWeek,* remembers, "Dr. Vagelos was an extraordinary leader, one of the finest and most admired corporate chieftains of his generation. What made him so remarkably effective in the job was his ability to relate to and engage with all of Merck's employees, from the scientists in the labs to the personal assistants behind office desks. During his stint as CEO, Merck was nothing less than an innovation machine, developing one blockbuster drug after another. Despite the company's incredible success, Dr. Vagelos stayed true to his own very high values of integrity and authenticity."

Athletic and rugged, with an easy smile and laugh, he seems as comfortable with production workers as with titans of industry and government. But he never looked comfortable with his own celebrity.

Roy Vagelos:

I achieved nothing by myself. Without great colleagues, family and friends I would have gone nowhere. No one has a monopoly on good ideas.

I always believed in dedication, zeal. Once you believe in something, go for it. When I was heading the research labs at Merck, I would often show up unannounced to ask what promising compounds our scientists were working on. One scientist would say something like, "I have 15 promising candidates for treating high blood pressure." That was ok, but what I really wanted to hear was, "we have 15 possible product candidates, but we have this one that looks great. We're doing the critical experiments to demonstrate that it will do the job." See the difference? In the second case, the researcher has the same number of compounds that show some anti-hypertensive effect but knows, as does the first researcher, that most will fail further safety or effectiveness tests in the test tube, animals or people. The second researcher is willing to bet the whole class of 15 compounds, to bet the farm, by choosing just one compound, based on chemical structure, history, and, always, some degree of instinct. He is willing to do the killer experiment.

Personal Branding Principle #1: Know who you are and what you stand for. Let it constantly be reflected in your performance, behavior and communication.

Roy Vagelos: "If you believe in something, go for it. Be willing to do the killer experiment."

Vagelos is all about zeal, ever the Greek American with the passion of Zorba. He loves Jersey Boys almost as much as he loves opera. He doesn't like to lose, whether at tennis or at drug discovery and development. The "killer experiment" is a kind of metaphor for his approach to living.

In 1975, as soon as he knew he was going to Merck Research Laboratories as second in command, Vagelos recruited Al Alberts, with whom he had worked at NIH and Washington University for 16 years, to head the basic research work with cholesterol. Company scientists had been studying the biochemistry of cholesterol for 20 years. Lipids (fats and other substances) and cholesterol were areas Alberts had been studying, and science was just beginning to point to a clear link between cholesterol levels and heart disease.

Alberts had finished the requirements for his doctorate, but never got around to finishing the dissertation. But Vagelos admired his dedication to science and his "tremendous skill and persistence at the lab bench." Alberts had been promoted up the professorial ranks at Washington University to associate professor with tenure, a rare accomplishment for a scientist without a PhD.

Roy Vagelos: "Anyone who knows Al knows he is special, a great scientist, someone you can always trust to do the lab work as perfectly and honestly as possible."

Together, the two new Merck scientists had absolutely zero experience with drug discovery, let alone development.

But Vagelos knew that many of history's greatest drugs, from aspirin to penicillin, were eventually shown to be so-called enzyme inhibitors, meaning they block the action of certain enzymes (large proteins) in the body that contribute to disease. For the next 19 years at Merck, he pushed his scientists to look for the enzyme that was causing the disease and then build compounds that might block it safely. And if the experimental drug did not have the promise of being significantly better than the ones already on the market—drop it, he would say.

Roy Vagelos: "I believed in this new, molecular targeting approach to drug discovery and development, and I considered it a big part of my job to enlist the support of all our scientists to that strategy. I wanted to convey a sense of unity and urgency."

"Roy was like an evangelist," Al Alberts remembers.

In 1978 the Alberts team identified, from a soil sample, an enzyme inhibitor they called lovastatin, which blocked the formation of cholesterol. With speed unusual for a new drug candidate, the Merck researchers demonstrated lovastatin to be highly effective in reducing cholesterol levels in the test tube and in animals, and its chemical structure indicated that it might be safe. So Merck began human trials in April 1980. Roy Vagelos had been at Merck just five years, and this already looked like a very significant new medicine.

Five months later, he ordered the trials to be stopped based on rumors—to this day unsubstantiated—that a similar compound had caused cancer in dogs in tests conducted by a company in Japan.

Both Vagelos and Alberts use the word "devastated" when referring to that day.

But Al Alberts was not convinced: "I thought the chemistry of lovastatin was right for reducing cholesterol in the body. I think that chemistry haunted Roy too."

In July 1982, in response to requests from physicians in Texas and Oregon, Merck made lovastatin available in tightly controlled trials in patients with such genetically high levels of cholesterol that family members were often dying in their 40s. Cholesterol levels dropped dramatically. So in August, after Merck researchers had completed animal tests demonstrating that lovastatin did not cause cancer in animals, Merck resumed human testing.

Roy Vagelos: "Al came to me, joking that he never had a doubt. I must say, he was persistent."

In August 1987, after some 30 years of Merck research, lovastatin, with the brand name Mevacor, was approved for marketing by the US Food and Drug Administration. Before then, the only cholesterol-lowering medicine available was a sandlike substance that smelled like rotten fish and had to be stirred with water and drunk. And it was not very effective.

"Before Mevacor," Vagelos said in an article he wrote for the journal *Science* (May 24, 1991), "no agent had ever effected such dramatic drops in cholesterol levels."

In 1994 Merck announced the results of "the killer experiment," having placed the enormous bet that cholesterol-lowering drugs would reduce heart disease and prolong life. They had tested Merck's second cholesterol-lowering drug, Zocor, which represented a step forward in therapy, in 4,400 patients with coronary heart disease, monitoring them over five years. The study showed that Zocor cut strokes by 28 percent, deaths by coronary blockage by 42 percent and overall mortality by 30 percent.

"The medical community," Roy Vagelos remembers, "was astonished."

Today's major cholesterol-lowering drugs, from Lipitor to Crestor, inhibit the same enzyme as does lovastatin and are called statins. Merck's newest cholesterol-lowering drug, Vytorin, is a combination of a statin and an inhibitor of cholesterol absorption. Tens of millions of patients have been treated with these medicines.

Does this mean that 30 percent of tens of millions of patients have lived longer than they would have?

"It is impossible to make such extrapolations," Al Alberts says. "But it is unarguable that millions have lived, are living, longer and better lives than they would have without the statins."

Would these drugs have eventually been developed had Dr. Vagelos not decided to resume human trials of Mevacor?

Roy Vagelos: "We'll never know. In any case, by the time I got to Merck I was not personally conducting laboratory research, although

I surely stayed involved. The breakthroughs with Mevacor, Mectizan and our important medicines for cardiovascular and other diseases came from our chemists, biochemists, pharmacologists, molecular biologists and other great scientists in our labs. I am not sure there was ever a better drug discovery and development group."

Personal Branding Principle #2: Communication is the lifeblood of an organization. Don't let sclerosis set in.

Roy Vagelos: "If you let people know you want to help them, most people will respond well, even to pressure to excel."

Al Alberts: "Roy has a remarkable ability to inspire. Put another way, he can haunt your dreams. He gets you to the point where you just don't want to let him down."

As Merck CEO, Roy Vagelos became known for supporting the development of people who were especially rigorous in their thinking, regardless of the jobs they held. His protégé Mary McDonald became general counsel, one of the few women in industry to hold the top legal spot at that time. Judy Lewent became the first woman chief financial officer of a Fortune 100 company.

Judy Lewent: "Roy always wanted to extend the boundaries of success, and not just in drug research. We needed to achieve the highest environmental and worker safety standards. He pushed for diversity in our workforce long before the term was popular. He made us all more competitive and he made competing fun. People wanted to work at Merck—discovering, developing and marketing great new medicines and doing all the collateral things better than anyone else. Under Roy, Merck was, in a real sense, Camelot."

Job applications increased severalfold during his tenure as CEO, and in 1991 every one of Merck's 37,700 employees received a stock option, extending that incentive farther in the ranks than any large firm had done before. Earnings statements and forecasts had to be as precise as possible. Not once during his tenure did the company restate a quarterly or annual earnings statement. Responsibility and circumspection were the communication guidelines long before there was the "forward-looking statement" now required by the US Securities and Exchange Commission.

A few years before his 1994 retirement from Merck, Vagelos was involved in the recruitment of Ken Frazier, a young African American lawyer, to Astra Merck, one of Merck's joint venture companies. Frazier, a Harvard lawyer, is the grandson of a man born into slavery.

"Ken has a remarkable life story," Vagelos says, "and he has a terrific personality, so it is hard not to like him as soon as you meet him. But what I found remarkable was the way he thinks about difficult challenges—like a scientist, with great rigor. It was clear that Ken had great leadership qualities, so the challenge was to be sure he was given the opportunity."

So in 1994, Vagelos promoted Ken Frazier to vice president of public affairs for Merck, where he would gain valuable leadership experience across the entire company. Vagelos's successors as CEO saw the same qualities, promoting Frazier to general counsel and into marketing and other leadership roles. In 2011 the Merck board of directors named him CEO and chairman of the board.

After Vagelos left Merck in 1994, the company experienced a series of problems. Several late-stage investigational medicines failed over the coming years. The company missed some earnings projections. In 2004, Merck voluntarily withdrew from the market the pain killer Vioxx, which was followed by a series of prominent product liability suits. Its reputation took a big hit.

"I think Merck is resurgent now," Vagelos says. "And I believe that Ken Frazier will do a great job."

TALK WITH ROY VAGELOS ABOUT REPUTATION, AND HE WILL SAY IT IS ALL ABOUT performance and behavior. Reluctantly, he will consent to the proposition that communication is a factor.

"Communication," he says, "is just something you do."

Truth be told, though, he is awfully good at it: "Keep it simple. That's key."

In 1989 there was a proposal in Washington to privatize the National Institutes of Health. The policy people for Merck and for the pharmaceutical industry group in Washington were formulating long position papers. Milt Freudenheim of the *New York Times* visited Merck headquarters to interview Roy Vagelos on Merck's growth prospects. To begin, Freudenheim asked, in a casual way, what he thought of the idea of privatization.

"I think it's a dumb idea," Vagelos said. In that instant, the heretofore arcane policy matter was settled, never to be resurrected.

Milt Freudeheim remembers him as being able to focus on what was important: "In the Vagelos era, Merck set the industry standard for pharma—research drove the business."

Roy Vagelos never liked distractions.

He believed in transparency long before it was a buzzword. He was the first CEO of a major pharmaceutical company to meet with AIDS activists. He gave Mike Waldholz of the *Wall Street Journal* wide access to Merck's HIV research, which then formed the basis for Waldholz's Pulitzer Prize–winning series.

When the company introduced its first anti-HIV investigational compounds for early human trials in November 1990, Vagelos understood the need to issue a press release. The AIDS community would learn of the trials because they had been following every step the company had taken in AIDS research since the beginning of the epidemic in 1981. Go ahead with a press release, he told his communication team, but keep it simple.

The one-page Merck press release issued on December 20, 1990, stated that the company was beginning early human safety trials of two compounds that would probably fail. And they did.

The AIDS virus proved much more difficult to defeat than early research had suggested. Many compounds, including several discovered by Merck, looked promising in early human trials, but the virus quickly developed resistance. Dr. Edward Scolnick, whom Vagelos had recruited from NIH to succeed him as head of research, himself recruited some of the world's best biomedical researchers.

The young Merck scientists would see their hopes elevated one day and dashed the next by the virus they called "that dirty little bastard." Vagelos and Scolnick shared their frustration and impatience. That led to Merck's leadership role in the 1993 formation of the Inter-Company Collaboration for AIDS Drug Development, an organization of 15 pharmaceutical firms that would share information and drugs for possible combination therapies. No one was quite sure if there had been such a coalition before. Finally, Merck's long and expensive effort would pay off within a year after Roy Vagelos left with the introduction of an antiviral treatment that would become an important part of HIV therapy.

Roy Vagelos: "A big part of the Merck history and reputation has always been the company's ability to communicate clearly on matters of health care."

Since 1899, Merck had published, on a not-for-profit basis, *The Merck Manual,* one of the most respected sources of medical information for doctors, nurses, pharmacists and other health-care professionals. In the late 1980s Merck Corporate Communications recommended that the company adapt that manual for lay people since thousands were purchasing it even though it was written in technical language.

The Merck law department objected, explaining that the company could lose its product liability defense, called "the learned intermediary defense," which had protected it against claims by anyone who might have suffered an adverse effect from one of the medicines in the *Manual,* whether from Merck or any other firm. The company had not communicated with the patient, the defense went, but with the "learned intermediary" (namely, the doctor) who had communicated with the patient. Publish a manual for lay people, and the door would be open to product liability suits.

Merck Corporate Communications persisted, since the desire for more health-care information was intensifying and Merck was best positioned to satisfy it. But the law department's argument was compelling. Finally, in 1993, Vagelos overruled the lawyers, giving the okay to proceed. *The Merck Manual, Home Edition,* was introduced in 1997. By 2011, the book was in three million homes in the United States and had been translated into a dozen languages.

When Merck formed a joint venture with Johnson & Johnson in 1989 to market over-the-counter versions of Merck's prescription medicines, Vagelos understood that communication issues would arise—who should say what and when? "Keep it simple," he told the communicators from both firms. Within weeks, the corporate communication folks at Merck and J&J wrote and agreed to the "Framework for Cooperation," which guided the joint venture for years to come.

"We will do our best to resolve issues at the communication level," it promised. The Framework was one page long.

In the early 1990s Merck announced that it would become the first major company to ban smoking not only in its buildings but on most of its property. The announcement declared it a done deal; Merck leadership had cleared this in advance with the union and groups of employees who had at first been resistant.

"It made no sense for a health-care company to have people smoking outside the entrances to our buildings," Vagelos says. The questions of civil liberties and worker and union rights had already been resolved.

Roy Vagelos: "Sometimes, it is simply a matter of doing the right thing, which can sound self-righteous, but it's true. I sometimes have a hard time understanding how so many leaders in government and industry say they faced these very difficult moral choices. I don't know that I ever faced a difficult problem that wasn't easily resolved in the end by asking, what is the right thing to do?"

In 1992, he pledged on behalf of Merck to keep its average US price increases at or below the Consumer Price Index.

Roy Vagelos: "Our marketing and finance people told me that 'you are leaving money on the table'. . . . But the CPI pledge was the right thing to do so we went ahead with it."

Cole Werble, publisher of the leading industry publication *The Pink Sheet*, remembers:

"Merck's competitors were not happy about what they called 'the Rahway Pledge,' because they then felt pressure to adopt the same policy. I remember thinking at that time that this was a kind of pricing collusion in the public interest. It was as if Dr. Vagelos got the CEOs in a room and told them that you, we, must cap our price increases—and none of us has a choice. I know that did not happen. As it turned out though, most of the major companies followed suit, taking the Rahway Pledge. Roy Vagelos deserved his reputation of being a maverick."

So, again, why is Roy Vagelos a great communicator? He is a very good writer and a good speaker, but that's only part of it. His strength has always been the one on one.

Judy Lewent: "He has a way of complimenting your work that is clearly genuine, and he can shoot you a look of disapproval that tells you that you are on the wrong track, without so much as one word. He is one of the best motivators I have ever known."

And he often does that by telling stories.

He knew by rote the history of Merck, back to its beginnings as a small apothecary in Darmstadt, Germany, in the 1600s, and when one of his executives did not seem to know or care about that history, Roy Vagelos would give that look which said "You'd better read up on your history." He would often quote George W. Merck, the founder of modern-day Merck, who said: "Medicine is for the people. If we have remembered that, the profits have followed."

Some senior executives at Merck during the Vagelos years would joke that when the debate on the executive committee became too heated, the person who invoked the George Merck quote first would win.

Roy Vagelos: "There's some truth to that."

One of his greatest tests as a communicator was the period of the few years leading up to the 1987 announcement that Merck would donate Mectizan to treat river blindness wherever it was needed for as long as it was needed. He met with world leaders from the health community, some of whom were cynical at best about the promise of Mectizan. He met with policy experts from the United States and Europe and with international aid organizations.

Bob Fluss, who coordinated the policy and communication initiatives for Merck and Mectizan leading up to the announcement of the donation, recalls:

> Roy came close to losing his patience more than once. Here you had
> a company whose existence is predicated on profits and the company
> was looking for ways to get a medicine it had spent years and mil-
> lions to develop to the people who needed it. One organization after
> another said "We don't have the budget." In one meeting a few leaders
> of the world health community intimated that our company could
> be subject to adverse publicity if the medicine was not donated to the
> poor countries where the disease was endemic. We had been going
> through a very deliberative and thorough process to come to the right
> decisions about Mectizan and I remember I was glad Roy was not
> there to hear this veiled threat. It would have infuriated him as it did
> all the Merck people at the meeting. But he heard about it later and
> had a few short words he would not want me to repeat.

As the 1980s passed, the company continued to do the human trials and all the regulatory filings necessary for approval of Mectizan, determined to show as much scientific rigor as it would for any new drug. In early 1987, the French regulatory authority, recognized as modern and rigorous, was getting ready to approve the drug for use in its former African colonies and for people in France who had lived there. There was still no international aid organization willing to take on the cost and logistical challenges of distribution.

At a Merck executive committee meeting in the summer, the CEO said, "That's enough. That's it. We will give it away."

Immediately, the company began to establish an expert committee of physicians, epidemiologists and government officials to establish and monitor protocols to ensure that Mectizan would get to the destinations intended and that patients would be recorded and monitored for once-a-year dosing. Vagelos helped recruit as head of the committee Dr. William Foege, who had led the vaccination program that defeated smallpox.

Roy Vagelos: "There was no choice but to develop Mectizan and to donate it."

River blindness results from infection by a parasite that is passed to people by the bite of a black fly that breeds near rivers. Microscopic when deposited in the skin, the parasite grows to feet-long lengths in the body. The disease causes itching so severe that it is not uncommon for those infected to scrub their skin literally to the bone. The torment was so bad and constant that people would commit suicide. Others, after years of being bitten and infected, would end up with the microscopic stage of the parasite lodged in their eyes, causing incremental blindness. It was not uncommon for most people over 40 in an African village to be blind.

Still, many others—both then and today—would consider donating Mectizan to be a choice.

In 2011, Roy Vagelos learned that a professor in California had asked a class of graduate business students what they would have done.

Roy Vagelos: "Thirty-eight of forty students said no—they would have held Mectizan until some organization bought it from us. Can you believe that? What does that say?"

The cover of the *New York Times Magazine* of January 8, 1989, showed a blind man in an African village being led by a boy on the other end of a cane. Reporter Erik Eckholm called Mectizan and the river blindness control project "one of the century's great medical triumphs."

Now, well into a new century, Mectizan remains one of the most remarkable medicines ever discovered. Imagine a drug that people in cities, villages or the bush can take just once a year to prevent or treat a disease that plagued their ancestors for centuries. And then go back to their homes right away, with very seldom an adverse reaction. (Imagine such a drug for cancer, or for diabetes.)

By 2010 Merck was donating Mectizan to treat about 100 million people a year in Africa. The drug has also proven effective in preventing lymphatic filiarisis, or elephantiasis, a disease in many ways as bad as river blindness.

Personal Branding Principle #3:
What goes around comes around.

Roy Vagelos: "People, organizations, even countries, have long memories."

Soon after arriving at the Merck research labs in 1975, Vagelos learned that Merck had worked with Selman Waxsman and Albert Schatz of Rutgers University after World War II to develop streptomycin, the first drug to treat tuberculosis effectively. When a TB epidemic struck Japan after World War II, the Japanese asked Merck for help. The company, realizing how impoverished the country was in the wake of the war, granted a royalty-free license. The Japanese then produced enough streptomycin and stopped the epidemic.

"Over the coming years," Vagelos said, "I noticed that our researchers seemed to be very well received by the Japanese."

Later, as CEO, he noticed that same kind of favorable prejudice toward anybody at Merck and a great receptivity to the company's proposals. That was significant because Merck was becoming increasingly global and Japan was the world's second largest prescription drug market.

Merck became more and more involved in Japan. In 1983 it purchased a 51 percent share in Banyu, becoming the first non-Japanese company to gain a major presence there. By the time Roy Vagelos left Merck in 1994, Merck, through Banyu, was well on its way to becoming a very successful competitor in the Japanese market. (In 2003, Merck acquired full ownership of Banyu.)

Roy Vagelos: "The people at Merck who made the decision to permit the Japanese to produce streptomycin, with no profits for the company, did it for the same reason that we, about 40 years later, would make the Mectizan decisions. There was no calculus that, over the long term, the company would be remembered—and rewarded. But that is what happened in Japan."

Stories! Family history, company history—it is all important, he says.

During World War II, Merck had been the first company to produce penicillin in large quantities. So the company was positioned, conditioned by history and culture, to respond when the tuberculosis epidemic struck Japan, even though the two countries had been mortal enemies a few short years earlier.

Today, now that Ken Frazier is CEO, Roy Vagelos is more aware of what is going on at Merck than he has been since retiring in 1994.

Roy Vagelos: "I have recently become reconnected to Merck and have lectured at the Merck Labs. I loved it. But we have our own great work going on now at Regeneron and I do not want to put anyone in a sensitive position. I cannot tell you though how happy I am to see Merck doing great things again. More great stories to come, I'm sure."

Ken Frazier: "My time working with and under Roy Vagelos has been invaluable. He has always emphasized what Merck stands for: translating cutting-edge science into medically important products and then finding innovative ways to get those products to those who need them. In other words, Roy has always shown how creating economic and shareholder value is completely complementary to and consistent with the social and medical value that is at the core of Merck's mission. As I travel the world, I am constantly reminded that his decision to donate Mectizan for river blindness literally ushered in a new era of global corporate responsibility. As Merck's new CEO, I have been subjected to a fair amount of scrutiny as well as some criticism. I feel fortunate to have frequent and easy access to Roy. When I call, he's always there to provide counsel and support. For that, I am immensely grateful."

On a recent trip to China, Roy Vagelos visited one of the plants that manufacture the vaccine against hepatitis B. Many of the Chinese scientists who have been involved since the Merck decision in 1989 to transfer the vaccine technology huddled near to meet and talk with him. They spoke of the 10 percent of Chinese infants who were infected before the vaccination program began, and how hepatitis B often causes serious disorders including cancer and liver failure over the long term. They knew that Merck had made no profit on the technology transfer. They knew that, in 2014, virtually all of China's 25 million newborns will be vaccinated.

Merck is expanding rapidly in China. It is building a new manufacturing facility in Hangzhou, near Shanghai, and is conducting large human trials in cooperation with Fuwai University and the Oxford Clinical Trials group.

Roy Vagelos: "Ken Frazier recently told me that Merck's sales in China have doubled in the last two years, making a significant contribution to Merck's sales growth. I wouldn't be surprised if someday, the same kind of turn of events happens for Merck in Africa and Latin America. It was possible 20 years ago for a company to do good and do well. I think it still is."

LESSONS

1. A company's value (market capitalization) is significantly affected by reputation. Does that say anything to any of today's executives about reputation management—that, just maybe, they should be actively practicing it?
2. The best way to manage an individual's or a company's brand (how they want to be perceived) as well as reputation (how others perceive them) is to manage the component parts: performance, behavior, communication and identity (character).
3. Communication should always be true to actual performance, behavior and what the organization stands for.
4. Once you find good people to work with, you have to simply trust them to do a good job. Roy Vagelos: "Any other approach to management and leadership is simply not rational."
5. Good communicators may not always be good leaders, but good leaders must be good communicators.
6. Personal Branding Principle #1: Know who you are and what you stand for. Let it constantly be reflected in your performance, behavior and communication.
7. Personal Branding Principle #2: Communication is the lifeblood of an organization. Don't let sclerosis set in.

8. Personal Branding Principle #3: What goes around comes around.
9. People, organizations and even countries can have long memories.
10. Success can take time.

FOUR

THE POWER OF PLANNING

Energy Man with a Plan

No Matter the Goal, Every Person
and Business Needs One

TRUE OR FALSE: AMERICA IS DEPENDENT ON FOREIGN OIL BECAUSE the country does not have enough energy resources of its own.

If this is false—and it is, starkly so—then why did America import nearly 60 percent of its oil in 2011? Why is the developed world so vulnerable to Iranian threats to blockade the Strait of Hormuz? Why is America habitually under the influence of OPEC and addicted to its oil?

That's easy, says T. Boone Pickens, billionaire tycoon, philanthropist, energy policy authority, activist and unabashed patriot: "For decades, America's political leadership has failed to tackle what I believe is one of the greatest threats ever to face this nation: our dependence on foreign oil. There has been no national energy plan."

No matter the goal, he says—and whether you're an individual entrepreneur, a small or large business or a government—"A fool with a plan can beat a genius with no plan."

In other words, if you don't know where you're going, you will invariably end up in the wrong place. Or, as in the case of America's no-policy energy policy, you could end up in a very bad and dangerous place.

Boone Pickens: "It is still not too late. But we don't have much time."

Pickens grew up in Holdenville, Oklahoma, a small agricultural community in the southeastern part of the state. His father was a landman in the oil industry.

He remembers the strength and wisdom of his father and mother. He remembers the struggles of his family and neighbors during the Great Depression, but he also remembers "always having food on the table in our house." Back then, most boys were content to let life happen to them. Not young Boone.

His first real business enterprise was a paper route. He realized he could make more money simply by adding more customers and working a little harder. He devised a plan to double the number of subscribers on his route by providing better service—throwing the paper closer to the door—and by coming up with a sales pitch for prospective customers. He knocked on every door he passed, thanking his existing customers and pitching his service to everyone else. He knew good word of mouth would make it easier for him to land new customers. So he set out to develop a reputation on the two streets that made up his paper route as the most dependable paperboy in Holdenville.

Within five years, his route grew from 28 daily papers to 156. With a profit of about one penny per paper, he saved close to $200. "It was my first experience in the takeover field: expansion by acquisition," he remembers.

This experience taught him the power of communication and reputation when linked to good performance and behavior.

When Boone was 16, the Pickens family moved from Oklahoma to Texas, but it did not take long for him to find himself back in Oklahoma, studying at Oklahoma A&M (now Oklahoma State University) toward a degree in geology. After graduation, he was introduced to the oil industry at Phillips Petroleum, where he worked for three years as a geologist before deciding to set out on his own.

With little money, he decided to learn all he could about the oil business. For the next two years, he worked as a consultant for oil companies in the Texas Panhandle. On the side, he put together drilling deals, modest at first, but soon numbering in the double digits.

Boone Pickens: "Back then, I was not alone in seeing so many opportunities in the oil industry. What gave me an advantage, I think, was the commitment to planning, constantly reassessing where I wanted to go and how to get there."

In 1956, at age 28 and with $2,000 in hand, he founded what would later become known as Mesa Petroleum, where he used his knowledge of geology to find oil and his skill as a salesman to make deals. Over the next several years, he built the Amarillo, Texas–based energy company into one of the biggest independent natural gas and oil producers in the nation. The company prospered and went public in 1964. Back then, the big guys running the giant oil companies did not see him coming.

Boone Pickens: "I love to make things happen."

He did just that at Mesa, pulling off a merger with a company 20 times bigger than his, Hugoton Production Company of Garden City, Kansas. That 1969 acquisition, which many industry peers thought could not be completed, launched his career as one of history's most successful corporate takeover artists. Yet the big guys still didn't take him seriously.

One acquisition led to another, each bolder than the last. Some observers quipped that the 1970s and 1980s were "easy Pickens." The big guys were finally beginning to hear footsteps.

Boone Pickens: "In each case, I looked for companies that were being poorly managed, to the detriment of their shareholders. I never went after any company without knowing what was wrong with it, how to change it and where to take it."

He relished the highly publicized boardroom brawls against such Goliaths as Phillips, Gulf and Unocal. He earned the label "corporate raider" from creative reporters and industry analysts. On December 23, 1983, *Fortune* magazine declared him "the most hated man in corporate America."

One of his most profitable ventures came from the 1984 merger of Gulf Oil and Chevron. He and a group of investors in Gulf earned $760 million, and Mesa netted $404 million. The treasurer for Gulf at the time, Cameron Payne, later said of T. Boone Pickens: "He's an audacious opportunist and a clever businessman who is able to see into the future and capitalize on it."

Boone Pickens: "Powerful people lose their power, and they are generally very unhappy about that. But no one can argue with the fact that I helped make the American oil industry more efficient. And that was very good for the country."

In 1996, he left Mesa. At age 68, with a relatively modest investment of $20 million, he founded an energy hedge fund, giving it the imprimatur of his initials, BP Capital. It took off from the start. Taking advantage of the rise of the energy sector in subsequent years, BP Capital rapidly grew into a multibillion-dollar fund.

He proved every bit as successful at finding lucrative investments as he was at finding oil. He'll be the first to tell you that when it came to making money, he was a late bloomer. He's made 90 percent of his fortune since he turned 75, a fortune he intends to give away. (He's already donated over a billion dollars to universities and charities.)

By 2007, Pickens had as deep a knowledge of other energy sources as he did of oil. His wife, Madeleine, was already tired of hearing him incessantly complain about the country's lack of an energy plan. He fervently believes the inaction of presidents and congresses on national energy policy for the past 45 years has put the country in great peril, and the American dream at risk for future generations. Well, do something about it, Madeleine told him.

He did.

By now he was 79, and his reputation had softened from corporate raider to astute businessman, philanthropist and energy-policy maven. He would put the weight of that reputation behind an audacious energy plan. He was confident that he could do what Washington had not.

The goal was easy for him to articulate to anyone who would listen. He expressed it in a militant tone, as befits any serious goal or objective: to create and foster the adoption of a national energy plan that will achieve energy independence for America within one decade.

He conceived the Pickens Plan out of sheer determination born of frustration. A realist, he knew the plan had to extend well beyond the 2008 and 2012 elections. He now had a new ambition, greater than any before—to get America out of the quicksand of stalling on energy policy and show Americans how they could become vastly more energy secure, if not energy independent.

The pillar of the plan is the knowledge that America still has abundant energy resources. When he first started saying that, he sounded as out of touch with reality as those who said in the 1950s, '60s, '70s and '80s that the Soviet Union would collapse under its own tyranny.

AMERICA'S ENERGY RESOURCES

His policy experts have the data on energy resources in America, and they present a compelling case.

In late 2007 and the spring of 2008, Pickens developed a multi-faceted plan for America's energy future. For months, he stress-tested the plan with key oil and gas industry officials and business and government leaders, including Warren Buffett, General Electric CEO Jeff Immelt, former New York Governor George Pataki and President George W. Bush.

It is an "all-American" plan, one that champions the use of all domestic resources in power generation and transportation. On the generation side, Pickens advocates renewables such as solar and wind. He defends coal as a power source, "as long as it's cleaned up." But on the transportation side—which accounts for two-thirds of total oil use—he proposes replacing OPEC's oil, diesel and gasoline with domestic natural gas.

Advances in drilling techniques have led to dramatic increases in natural gas resources and production. It has been demonstrated that natural gas can be extracted in a way that is physically and environmentally safe. The magnitude of the reserve base—and its potential impact in transportation—is profound. Converting America's eight million heavy-duty and fleet vehicles to compressed or liquefied natural gas vehicles—just that one action—could cut OPEC imports in half in just five years.

Boone Pickens: "The facts are on our side, but the noise is so intense that it's hard to get our messages through. Politicians have their own agendas. Conservationists and environmentalists do too. For us to cite the fact that the United States has more than enough energy is not to say that there are not environmental and conservation concerns. On the other hand, in order to move forward, all we need do is acknowledge that we have the resources and that we have to find the best ways to utilize them in the right combinations and under the right safeguards. We have to declare our energy independence."

All he needed was a plan—and a voice. During the stress-testing phase, Pickens heard heard Fox News' Roger Ailes say something that, though hyperbolic, rang true: "Educate the public on how much natural gas we have. Then find out who's against it. Then shoot them."

When first formulating the Pickens Plan, he applied leadership, communication and planning principles. What does it take to energize Americans on the issue of energy? What is the right message to penetrate the clutter and noise during election years and the years in between? How can we move energy into the national conversation? How can we build an army of motivated advocates?

PLANNING FOR A PLAN

A good plan starts with thinking like a military strategist. Indeed, the terms used in a communication plan derive from the military:

- Goal: a generalized statement of specific objectives—what you want to achieve.
- Strategy: how to get there; the umbrella approach for the tactics or tools; the way to organize the tactics.
- Tactics: specific communication techniques and tools that will be employed to convey the messages—blogs, press releases, tweets, editorial board visits.

The language a person uses in speaking or writing about a plan reflects how clearly he or she is thinking: for instance, one *accomplishes* a goal or objective; one *carries out* or *implements* a strategy; one *employs* or *uses* tactics.

Taking a military example: the *goal* would be to win the war; an *objective* would be to win one battle; the *strategy,* to take the hill; and the *tactics* would be rifles, grenades, missiles and so on. (The best source for how to think like a military strategist is the 1832 book *On War* by the Prussian General Carl von Clausewitz.)

A good plan starts with excellent leadership. Pickens recognized the Herculean task ahead. He knew he needed to assemble the best political, communication, research, creative and online strategists. Since he was about to invest over $50 million of his own money in the campaign, he consulted with several business colleagues and political leaders to help identify the best talent. He relied on his vice president of public affairs at BP Capital, Jay Rosser, to assemble the team.

Early on, Rosser, a trusted counselor to Pickens and a seasoned public affairs and media professional, reached out to Tom Synhorst, managing partner and chairman of DCI Group, a public affairs firm in Washington, DC. Synhorst became the quarterback. He and Rosser assembled a powerhouse research, creative, public relations and online team, consisting of:

- DCI, a political consulting and lobbying firm with a knack for creating grassroots organizations and recruiting third-party allies to advocate for a cause or an issue, which signed up on the spot after hearing Mr. Pickens's vision for the campaign.
- Sloane & Company, Point Blank Public Affairs and Rich Galen, media relations and earned media strategists.
- Network Relations and North Bridge Communications, grassroots strategists.
- Villageous, Haddad Media and Eric O'Keefe, digital advocates.
- Gogerty Marriott, the Mercury Group, Peter Hart and Joe Slade White, research, creative and paid media strategists.

Boone Pickens: "If you can find someone who can do the job better than you, hire that person."

THE PICKENS PLAN

THE PROBLEM

America has been facing an energy crisis for almost half a century. OPEC turned off the pipeline in the late 1970s with an embargo, which meant little oil but lots of inflation and unemployment for the United States. It could happen again. Pickens points to the ever-intensifying tension in the Middle East to underscore his concerns. If Iran were to close the Strait of Hormuz, a critical shipping channel between the Persian Gulf and Indian Ocean through which roughly 40 percent of the world's oil passes, it would trigger a historic rise in energy prices that could paralyze America's economy.

How dependent is America on OPEC and foreign oil? Since 1976, factoring in military and other costs, the United States has spent $7 trillion on OPEC oil. That's roughly half the US national debt.

Pickens has always been a master at using data to start the conversation—and to startle his listeners. Indeed, communication theorists suggest that one of the best ways to overcome cognitive dissonance—people's tendency not to listen to arguments that are unpleasant to them or out of line with their existing beliefs—is to startle.

Boone Pickens: "Americans simply do not want to think about the fact that our country's very survival is threatened."

Without a plan, he knew the country would continue to spend billions on foreign oil instead of pursuing cleaner domestic energy resources including natural gas, wind, solar, clean coal and geothermal, as well as America's own oil. He also viewed the billions being spent to purchase oil from other countries as an "insane" transfer of wealth. Without a change in direction, America was headed for economic crisis—and worse.

The idea of securing America's energy and economic future via a region of the world historically cloaked in instability and turmoil was a message that Pickens believed would resonate. But it needed testing.

RESEARCH

Research is both the alpha and the omega of the planning process. It was the first step in constructing and introducing the Pickens Plan in 2008. For the Pickens Plan team, it meant conducting hundreds of focus groups across the country and testing dozens of messages and commercials.

Jay Rosser: "We knew that elected officials respond to constituents, and that what happens back home does matter to people in state capitals and Washington. Our team knew if we could inform individual Americans of the seriousness of the issue, they would become engaged and then involved. Their political leaders would then listen."

Focus groups showed that Americans were mainly concerned about the *price* of energy. For many, the energy issue boiled down to the cost of a gallon of gasoline. They had little sense of what factors impact that price. They knew about OPEC and, back in 2007 and 2008, were unsettled about the Iraq War. Older participants in the focus groups remembered with great detail the effects of the Arab embargoes of the 1970s. They remembered waiting in long lines to buy ten gallons of gas at prices twice as high as they had ever paid before. Younger participants were awakened to the issue by such stories.

As the participants discussed energy, they became frustrated when it dawned on them that the federal government had done nothing in decades to lessen the threat of dependency on oil from foreign sources, primarily OPEC. They got angry. That was good.

It quickly became clear that the best way to create a compelling conversation on energy was to frame it as an economic and security issue—"Our way of life is threatened and our destiny is in the hands of people who are hostile to the democratic beliefs and principles upon which our country was founded."

The research confirmed the team's belief that energy was a bi-partisan issue. Republicans and Democrats, rural and urban, energy proponents and environmental proponents were all united behind the idea of making America energy independent.

GOAL

To create and foster the adoption of a national energy plan that will achieve energy independence for America within one decade. (A more specific target, an objective, falls under the goal.)

STRATEGY #1—CREATING THE CONVERSATION

In 2008 Pickens made it clear to his team that he wanted energy to loom much larger in the national conversation. He wanted then-presidential candidates Barack Obama and John McCain discussing energy, detailing their ideas and, hopefully, offering a plan—a real plan. For too long, Americans had accepted talk as action on energy, says Pickens.

Tom Synhorst agreed. A master of the message, he knew that to win this battle, Americans must understand how the lack of an energy plan impacted them and put their way of life in jeopardy.

Tom Synhorst: "It's important to get both the policy and the politics right when it comes to a public issue such as energy. You must find the sweet spot—frame the issue and define it in the most favorable terms—find the place of mutual agreement."

While the Pickens Plan aimed to create a national conversation on energy, the team felt the plan must have points of interaction with the public in order to engage them and spur them to action. The plan was evolving at a time when communication via the Internet was soaring. While it's a foregone conclusion today that issues campaigns must have a digital component, the Pickens Plan in 2008 was charting new frontiers in cyberspace. Today, its online activities are viewed as a model of high-tech and high-impact advocacy with elected officials and the general public.

Immediately, tens of thousands of Americans, young and old, rich, middle class and poor, took to social media and began conversations via Twitter, Facebook, LinkedIn and blogs influenced by well-honed messages crafted by the communication team, aimed at winning minds and provoking actions. The digital team was ready. They monitored social media sites, created content on the Pickens Plan website and engaged with its audience. Dealing directly with people through social media helped the team monitor and adjust its strategies and messages in real time.

STRATEGY #2—GET AMERICANS TO DECLARE

The idea was to get people to sign up to support the Pickens Plan by actually taking a pledge. This is the same strategy that has proven so effective for organizations like Weight Watchers and Alcoholics Anonymous: in order to join, one must take a pledge. Declare!

Boone asked the public—and public officials—to commit to a pledge to reduce the nation's use of foreign oil by 30 percent within a decade.

TACTICS

The team put in place an extensive unpaid or earned (press) and paid (marketing and advertising) media campaign, starting with a major press conference in New York on July 8, 2008, for influential members of key media outlets and bloggers. The press conference was the launchpad for a national conversation on energy security. The call was for action and substantial progress, all within ten years.

As Yogi Berra said, "It gets late early around here."

The campaign included a series of well-timed earned media appearances, executed alongside a carefully created barrage of paid media spots.

The New Media World. The center of the Pickens Plan universe is its website. The team found that using technology (digital video, real-time communications, blogs, widgets and downloads, RSS feeds, audience engagement and so on) to identify and educate was the best way to build a broad conversation with maximum impact.

The team assembled at the website for instructions and conversation. Pickens even called the people who signed up "the Army."

He worked the Army hard. As its commander, he presided over online post-presidential debate sessions discussing key aspects of the energy dialogue.

But online advocacy, for all its strengths, cannot work in isolation. It must be part of an integrated effort.

Grassroots. Behind the scenes, a finely tuned and sophisticated grassroots operation, much like a presidential campaign, used direct mail, phone banks and local earned and paid media to make sure that crowds appeared and the local media covered the events. This targeted outreach inspired people to take action. They went to the website to sign up and found the tools to engage in an influential campaign.

Coalition Building. Pickens and team recognized the importance of coalition building and powerful third-party advocates. The team flight-tested the Pickens Plan with the likes of Ted Turner, Robert

Kennedy Jr. and then-president of the Sierra Club, Carl Pope, who particularly embraced the wind and solar component of the plan. There was something for everyone.

Tour de Pickens. Pickens has six decades of experience in the energy industry, and his populist appeal rests in his intelligence and quick wit. He set out to alter the national narrative on energy. The year-long series of strategic town hall meetings across the United States, which became known as Tour de Pickens, featured him as the main advocate of energy independence. At every turn, the team directed participants to the website to join the Pickens Energy Army, to lead the charge for energy independence among their friends and families.

Capitalizing on his popularity as a business maverick who stood up for shareholder rights in the late 1970s and early 1980s, Pickens's team initiated an aggressive earned-media campaign. They injected him into the national dialogue through an expansive program that included satellite media interviews, national morning and late-night show appearances, localized op-eds and editorial board meetings, sessions with national political and energy bloggers, and publicized debates with Pickens Plan critics.

Traditional Media. Pickens met with the editorial boards at the nation's most influential news organizations, including the *New York Times,* the *Wall Street Journal,* the *Washington Post,* the *Los Angeles Times,* the *San Francisco Chronicle,* the *Chicago Tribune,* the *Houston Chronicle* and the *Dallas Morning News.*

As former US Speaker of the House Tip O'Neill observed, "All politics is local." In a move reminiscent of old-fashioned campaigning techniques, Pickens barnstormed America like a modern-day Harry Truman on a whistle-stop tour. Hundreds, sometimes thousands, gathered to hear him outline his plan in an unscripted setting where his personal dedication to the cause was clear. Often governors, senators and members of Congress introduced him. They recognized that Pickens's message and plan had traction with the public and it was to their benefit to jump on board.

AUDIENCES

The team devoted much of its initial planning to formulating the right messages and adapting them for distinct audiences. They realized that the messages had to be personal and credible and had to resonate with the various stakeholder groups. The messages also had to work in today's fragmented media environment, where it is more challenging than ever to penetrate the clutter.

MESSAGE #1—THE FIGHT FOR AMERICAN INDEPENDENCE.

This is a big country, with 350 million people, and a lot of conversations take place every day. Solving America's energy crisis will not happen overnight, but creating a conversation about the energy crisis and providing a sensible, understandable solution that a broad cross section of Americans can endorse is key. Pickens wanted his energy plan to become "household," meaning it would evolve to the point where America's energy future was constantly discussed at the dinner table, at work and via social media (today's version of the office water cooler, only with a lot more room to gather and a lot more chatter.)

This message would be of particular interest to families concerned about rising gasoline prices, America's national energy security and the future of the country.

MESSAGE #2—"IF IT'S AMERICAN, I'M FOR IT."

As part of the strategy, Pickens and his team exercised great care in not playing favorites among energy sources. All that mattered to them was whether it was American. They made that abundantly clear during an exchange between Pickens and a member of the audience at a town hall meeting in Kansas, chronicled by the editor of *The Land Report* magazine, Eric O'Keefe.

O'Keefe reported that the biggest applause during the Kansas town hall meeting hosted by then-governor of Kansas Kathleen Sebelius happened when Pickens was asked about fuel cells and alternative energies. O'Keefe painted the picture as follows: "Caught flat-footed, he admits his ignorance and then quickly parries with a question of his own about the energy source. 'Is it American?' he asks. When informed that it is, he responds, 'Then I'm for it. I'm for anything American.' The crowded hall bursts into cheers."

He is "ignorant." Like a fox.

MESSAGE #3—WHY FUND BOTH SIDES OF A WAR?

During the focus group, a powerful message emerged—Americans are tired of funding both sides of the war. Early on, Jay Rosser coined the phrase that was to define the campaign: OPEC oil purchases constituted "the greatest transfer of wealth in human history." Worse still, according to Pickens, was the fact that much of that oil money landed in the hands of terrorists and others hostile to American ideals.

MESSENGERS

All the team members would be messengers. But there was never any doubt that Pickens would be out in front. He is very well known in America and is considered a business leader with a decisive, no-nonsense edge. People admire his philanthropy as well. They admire the fact that he has been funding the Pickens Plan with his own money. He is likable, believable and credible—everything you would want as the face of a campaign.

Pickens knows energy. More important, he has a well-researched and well-conceived plan to lead America to energy independence.

He articulates it clearly, and his homespun, candid conversational style connects with diverse audiences.

The whiteboard presentation he used at the July 8, 2008, press conference in New York is now trademark Pickens. Like a general standing before his troops, he outlined in graphic detail how America could attain energy independence, averting economic peril—and a major threat to national security.

BUDGET

When all is said and done, Pickens's total investment in his crusade approached $100 million, with more than half focused on paid media. While that paid media campaign dominated the airwaves for more than a year, it was his Army's outreach initiatives and the earned media campaign—i.e., public relations—that maintained steady pressure on Washington decision makers. And in the end, natural gas legislation designed to implement key pillars of the Pickens Plan had more than 180 House sponsors, split almost equally along party lines—proof of its bipartisan appeal.

THE POWER OF THE TRUTH

Today, public awareness of natural gas as a transportation fuel alternative to OPEC oil/diesel/gasoline is at an all-time high, and engine manufacturers, automakers, truck manufacturers and fleets have begun making the transition. President Obama embraced it in a 2012 speech. That said, legislation in the House has stalled, and, when presented as an amendment to the Transportation Bill in the Senate, it failed 51–47 (needed 60).

"Where I'm from in Southeastern Oklahoma, and in the big 12, 51 beats 47 every day. Washington's an odd place to do business," Boone says.

Inevitably, the success of the Pickens Plan will be just as dependent on the facts underpinning the plan as on the effectiveness of its communicators.

Pickens knows that America cannot shut off the spigot on fossil fuels—at least not within the next few decades—without risking an economic apocalypse. He also knows that wind and solar don't get to the heart of the OPEC dependence problem because they are not used as transportation fuels. Also, the economic collapse in late 2008 made wind and solar, which are priced off the margin, less economical than natural gas, which itself had collapsed in price. Still, he says, wind and solar will be a key part of America's energy future, and it's best to lay that foundation now.

Pickens learned firsthand the economic perils of renewable energies, having invested more than $150 million in wind energy projects that were all but stymied by the collapse in natural gas prices. Still, going forward, he says, low natural gas prices will be a key driver (no pun intended) of the transition to energy independence.

After all, he owns a 68,000-acre ranch in the panhandle of Texas where the wind blows often and at high speeds. The sun shines hard as well. Beneath the ground of his Roberts County, Texas ranch are oil and gas. It was here that the Pickens Plan percolated throughout 2007 and 2008, while he was quail hunting or surveying his vast spread, which he affectionately calls Mesa Vista because of the breathtaking views.

Pickens's willingness to embrace wind caught the attention of Pulitzer Prize–winning *New York Times* journalist Thomas Friedman, who described him as the "green billionaire oilman now obsessed with wind power." Indeed, Pickens says, without meaning any hyperbole, America can become "the Saudi Arabia of wind and natural gas."

All along, the Pickens team realized they needed support throughout the country. For instance, the solar energy industry is big in the western United States. Already, solar panel farms in the Nevada countryside are supplying energy to Las Vegas.

Boone Pickens: "You can't power an 18-wheeler using a battery—you need natural gas. America is awash in a sea of natural gas."

Advances in drilling techniques—some controversial among environmentalists—have opened up vast reservoirs of natural gas embedded in shale rock deep below the surface of the earth. America has the resources to transition—within just a few years' time—large truck fleets from diesel to natural gas in compressed (CNG) and liquefied (LNG) form. Pickens points out that such a transition would lead to a second industrial revolution and create more than 400,000 badly needed jobs in America.

Hydraulic fracturing, or fracking, a process using mostly water and sand (98 percent) and certain fluids combined with high pressure to detach natural gas molecules from shale formations deep below the surface, has become controversial among environmentalists. Their main complaint is that the process releases hazardous materials into otherwise clean water. However, the executive director of the Environmental Protection Agency, Lisa Jackson, said she believes the process can be carried out safely with the right rules and oversight. Studies are showing that the problems, especially contamination of drinking water, may not be caused by the hydraulic fracturing process, but poor well design. States such as Pennsylvania have developed rules and regulations to govern drilling and production activities.

The record-low natural gas prices of 2012 are the direct result of oversupply created by the effectiveness of the horizontal drilling and hydraulic fracturing technology. The low prices have spurred an industry renaissance in American manufacturing, as companies move operations back to America due to the favorable economics. In many parts of the country, including large swaths of Pennsylvania, the natural gas industry is booming.

Today, American truck and auto manufacturers are putting more funds into research and development for CNG and LNG trucks and cars. Major companies such as AT&T and UPS are converting more of their fleets to run on CNG. Congress is considering the Natural Gas Act to spur a quicker transition to natural gas as a transportation fuel for heavy trucks.

Pickens and his team have recruited coalition partners from across the political and policy spectrum. These partners include some unexpected bedfellows, such as environmental advocacy and energy advocacy organizations. Through the careful crafting of the right message, knowledge of the policy positions of all parties involved, including opposing environmentalists, and the precise execution of the broad and deep plan, the Pickens team has found the "sweet spot."

The Pickens Plan website remains active and influential today. It has become a powerful advocacy tool and is credited with persuading politicians, including President Obama, to embrace increased use of American-produced natural gas, particularly as a transportation fuel for large trucks.

THE PICKENS PLAN—RESULTS AT LAUNCH PLUS FOUR

The team launched the Pickens Plan in July 2008. By October 1, the results showed: energy was part of the conversation in the presidential campaign. Within four months, 250,000 Americans had signed on to the plan.

Back then, both presidential candidates met with Pickens to discuss his plan—sound evidence that the Pickens Plan was impacting the conversation on energy at the highest levels.

In 2009, the Pickens Plan was presented with the Association of Political Affairs Professionals award for Best Public Affairs Campaign of the Year.

In 2012, the Pickens Army consists of over 1.5 million people, enough to sway a presidential election, among other opportunities.

US PRESIDENT BARACK OBAMA: "T. BOONE PICKENS, WHO MADE HIS FORTUNE in the oil business—and I don't think anybody would consider him unfriendly to drilling—was right when he said that this is one emergency we can't drill our way out of. We can't place our long-term bets on a finite resource that we only control 2 percent of."

R. James Woolsey, former director of the CIA: "We should pay attention to T. Boone Pickens's recommendations to switch to natural gas for fleet vehicles such as buses, and for interstate trucking. Buses and trucks are easily modified to run on natural gas and would only require new pumps at a few central locations and interstate truck stops."

Jon Stewart, satirist: "Boone Pickens, I feel like right now, I and the rest of my audience would follow you out of the building. . . . I'm literally like sir, where do we go sir? I'm reporting for duty."

Al Gore, former US vice president: "United States of America, our country, is the only nation that can lead the world when a crisis like this looms. And in order to lead the world, we have to restore the momentum and the can-do spirit that—Boone Pickens exemplifies this—let's go and let's do this."

Carl Pope, former head of the Sierra Club: "To put it plainly, T. Boone Pickens is out to save America."

LESSONS

1. Research is the alpha and omega of the planning process.
2. Trying to tell large groups anything in this Age of the Conversation is usually a waste of time.
3. Getting people to declare is a great way of gaining participation: take the pledge.

4. The integrated communication campaign comprises four kinds of media: traditional, new, paid (advertising) and earned (public relations).
5. Align stakeholder groups and messages.
6. Allot enough time for success.
7. Precedent: there is always one out there somewhere. Ignore it at your peril.
8. If they won't even pay attention, shock 'em.
9. Your success will ultimately be in direct proportion to the power of your case and your strength as a communicator.
10. Boone Pickens: "A fool with a plan can outsmart a genius with no plan any day."

FIVE

THE POWER OF REPUTATION

How the Pros at J&J Do It,
In Good Times and Bad

RAY JORDAN, THE CHIEF COMMUNICATION OFFICER AT JOHNSON & Johnson, the world's largest health-care company, approaches reputation the same way he did math and psychology at Yale: through measurement, analysis and dedication. Where others see a complex, intangible asset, he sees an asset as real and definable as any—an asset that must be carefully managed.

At its core, he says, reputation is about identity—what the individual or organization, large or small, stands for. Despite what many observers have called "tumultuous times" resulting from a series of consumer drug recalls that no one would have expected from this company, Ray Jordan says that J&J's identity has been intact for 126 years.

The three Johnson brothers who founded the firm in 1886 in New Brunswick, New Jersey, where its world headquarters is today, had been captivated by the teachings of Joseph Lister, who had embraced Louis Pasteur's theory that invisible germs cause disease. Hence the company's first products, which included sutures and surgical dressings.

Robert Wood Johnson II, the son of one of the founding brothers, had served as a brigadier general in the US Army during World War II. Upon returning home to the family business, he became the evangelist for the Credo, which he had written in 1943. He described its basic principle: "Take care of the customers first, then our employees and then our communities, and the shareholders will get a fair return."

The first chief scientific officer for the company was Fred Kilmer, a New Brunswick retail pharmacist who also became the chief communicator for the young company. His eloquence in talking about the business values that would later become the Credo presaged the eloquence of his son, the poet Joyce Kilmer.

Today as then, new employees learn about the Credo, which hangs prominently and ubiquitously at J&J sites worldwide, as it does in the Kilmer Museum at J&J headquarters. Employees learn that the greatest test of the company's allegiance to it came in 1982 and 1986 with the Tylenol tampering cases, which caused the deaths of eight people from cyanide poisoning. Then-CEO Jim Burke decided to recall Tylenol capsules from every store and distribution point, using all available people and resources to retrieve it.

The Tylenol franchise was a significant part of the company's revenues. The US Food and Drug Administration and the Federal Bureau of Investigation were not convinced that a total Tylenol recall was necessary. But Jim Burke decided to do it anyway. Some industry analysts predicted that J&J could not rebound from the recall.

Burke's response to all the praise that followed, including being honored by President Ronald Reagan, was that he would accept praise for the people of Johnson & Johnson who had supported and implemented the recalls. But he did not deserve it, he said, because he simply had no choice: the Credo dictated his decision. Employees, communities and shareholders were important, but second to, as the first sentence of the Credo states, "the doctors, nurses and patients . . . mothers and fathers and all others who use our products and services."

By September 1983, Johnson & Johnson had regained Tylenol's share of the pain reliever market. (Revenues lost through the second recall were regained within months.)

Ray Jordan: "The key components of a company's reputation are the same now as they were back in 1986 and all the way back to 1886: performance, behavior and communication. They are the proof points for your character. However, organizations can and will make mistakes in those areas. But your character, your identity is inviolable. If you start compromising your identity, it's a slippery slope. Think about it: in a large organization, you have to have thousands, tens of thousands of employees standing up for what your organization is and what it stands for. To think about reputation that way is to never become complacent about it."

Ray Jordan is only the third chief communication officer at Johnson & Johnson since the position was formed in 1957, following Larry Foster, 1957–1990, and Bill Nielsen, 1990–2004. He thinks his predecessors did "a stunning job" helping to build one of modern history's most revered and valuable reputations. When he became CCO, he inherited stewardship of that reputation, sharing accountability with all J&J leaders, which they in turn shared with then-CEO and chairman Bill Weldon.

Ray Jordan: "Many chief communication officers say they cannot control most things that go on in their companies—and of course there is a lot of truth in that. But, it would be a mistake to conclude that therefore they are not accountable for reputation.

That is a recipe for disaster. As a leader at Johnson & Johnson, I accept accountability for the J&J reputation and will do all I can to protect and enhance it."

For Jordan's first five years it was relatively smooth sailing. Then, beginning in 2009 and continuing for over two years, J&J suffered a series of consumer product recalls, voluntary and precautionary, in product lines that were relatively small in terms of company revenues (less than 2 percent). They were the result of significant manufacturing issues, but the product issues themselves were relatively benign. Still, the recalls became very big and bad news, inside and outside the company.

Ray Jordan: "Much commentary was unfair, but criticism was warranted. J&J employees, from entry-level folks to our senior management, were more upset than anyone."

To understand why, one must understand the backstory.

The legendary company, as aggressive as any in the health-care business, had been known for an understated, circumspect, deliberate approach to communications—"slow and steady as she goes." Even before he moved into the CCO's office at world headquarters in New Brunswick, Jordan decided to hang on to the "steady" part—it fit his personality and the J&J culture—but abandon the "slow." The company was thriving in each of its three business segments—consumer, prescription medicines and medical devices and diagnostics. What's more, as those businesses expanded worldwide, more and varied groups of constituents—government, policy makers, consumer activists, nongovernmental organizations, even "mommy bloggers," were emerging in the new media world, seeking a stake of one kind or another in the burgeoning health-care conglomerate.

Fresh out of the gate in 2004, Jordan started building a stronger communication organization to support the worldwide network of companies, already numbering over 200, that operated pretty much independently within the decentralized framework of Johnson &

Johnson. At the same time, he and his team worked to ensure that both the employees in the individual operating companies and those in J&J corporate understood that there is one monolithic Johnson & Johnson value system: the Credo—which decrees that the company's first responsibility is to patients and customers, and then to employees, communities and shareholders.

Ray Jordan: "Some people think of our Credo as a mission statement, which by definition would make it aspirational. It is not. It is the standard by which we must work every single day."

Well into 2009, he proceeded as planned, staffing the three main business segments with a top communicator who reported to both the respective business leader and to him. By then virtually all the larger operating companies, numbering some two dozen with operations in 60 countries, had a communication function.

More and more of those communication officers were reporting to senior business leaders and participating in global management boards. Their assessments as leaders were based on their contributions to their businesses, not merely on their communication skills; those skills were the price of entry.

Jordan established a pioneering social media strategy for J&J (which would later be recognized as Social Media Company of the Year by Dose of Digital, an influential blog that promotes improving health care through digital technology). "Slow" was definitely out.

Jordan gained a reputation for developing and supporting his people. He established a capabilities and career development model for midlevel communicators and launched the Academy for Communication Excellence & Leadership (ACCEL) to foster the professional growth of J&J communicators worldwide. He became one of the public relations profession's most influential people, according to *PR Week* magazine, and was widely admired by peers. Most importantly, he had easy and frank access to any member of the company's C-suite.

Ray Jordan: "Our worldwide network of professional communicators exists primarily to support the operating companies. Each communicator is expected to be a strategist, helping to grow the products, services, and reputations of his or her company."

Jordan worked closely with the communication heads of the three business segments. It was their responsibility to ensure that the product, people or reputational issues that should percolate up to corporate did so in a timely fashion.

This highly unusual decentralized model had been serving J&J well for decades. The consumer business was thriving, with its heritage baby business contributing in an outsized fashion to the corporate identity and reputation. The mother-infant bond made women's loyalty to J&J unusually strong—otherworldly to cynics, sacred to J&J employees. Ray Jordan had the data showing that no other major company engendered such feelings of caring and trust.

The prescription medicines segment was also thriving, with products for mental illness, HIV, cancer and immune diseases. In the devices and diagnostics business, there were new, life- saving products for surgery, orthopedics and other uses.

As the company approached the new decade, it was poised for unprecedented growth. The R&D budget of $7 billion for 2010 would ensure continued innovations in all three business segments.

From day one, reputation was a key focus for Ray Jordan. He knew that a company has only one reputation, which is the sum of the images or views that the various groups or constituencies have of it. What drives those views for one group (earnings growth for securities analysts, for instance) may be different for another (carbon emissions for environmental activists).

"Messages should be distinct for distinct groups," he says, "but never in conflict."

He knew what each group wanted from J&J, felt about J&J, liked or disliked about J&J. He knew which groups would care that the company was investing $7 billion in research and which groups might become disengaged by the very use of the word "innovation." Very important, he knew what actions had to be taken before his group could communicate—"Action is key," goes the Jordan mantra—and that meant he and his communication leadership team needed engagement in business decisions before they were made.

Adding complexity was the long list of operating company names, some much more overtly associated with the parent company than others: DePuy and Cordis in the diagnostics business, Ortho and Jansen in pharmaceuticals, McNeil in consumer products. Initiatives were being planned, especially in the pharmaceuticals business, to streamline the identities of the various entities. How did their individual company reputations affect the J&J reputation, and vice versa? Which groups, stakeholders or constituencies even cared about the link?

Luckily, Ray Jordan is good at distilling simplicity from complexity. The most important groups would always be, he believed, those mentioned in the Credo—patients and customers, employees, communities and shareholders, in that order. Yet he was constantly dealing with emerging stakeholder groups as they grew more powerful.

Ray Jordan: "My job at J&J has always been challenging, never easy or routine. But for the first several years, the news from the business was, on balance, very good and supportive of our reputation."

He loved his work, does today more than ever, he says, and was able to maintain deep family ties with his wife, Karen, of 38 years, and his four grown sons. As 2010 approached, and he approached his late 50s, life and work were sweet.

The company had become a leading voice in the United States and abroad on all kinds of issues impacting health care. J&J was an early and vocal supporter of "thoughtful" health-care reform, having published a statement of its position on global reform called "The

Promise of Health Care." For people in developing countries, J&J committed to research into treating or preventing ancient scourges like malaria. In industrialized countries, the company took advantage of opportunities to expand its reputation.

It became a major sponsor of the 2008 Summer Olympic Games in Beijing. No matter the initiative, Corporate Communication identified and mapped the risks and mitigated them with extensive public-policy engagement. China's humanitarian challenges were, to many critics, reason not to support the Olympics. But the J&J business was growing rapidly in China. The company's calculus was that it could do more good over the long term by working with the government and the people of the country.

An implied message of the Credo is that employees must remain ever watchful. And so it was in 2006 that an employee reported to corporate that a subsidiary might have made payments to doctors in Greece so that they would use J&J's orthopedic products. As soon as the senior executives at New Jersey headquarters learned of this complaint, they engaged outside counsel to conduct an investigation, and the results of that investigation were disclosed to the US Department of Justice and the Securities and Exchange Commission. The company would later pay $78 million in fines, disgorgement and interest to settle issues involving payments to physicians in Greece, Poland and Romania, and payments to the government of Iraq in connection with the Oil-for-Food Program.

"This was an embarrassment for J&J," Ray Jordan says, "but the company reported the offense as we learned of it and did everything possible to prevent it from happening again. In a workforce of over 100,000 people—the population of a city—people will sometimes do the wrong thing.

"In public relations, it is important to get caught doing the right things. But when things go wrong, it is important to disclose them."

In 2009, reports began surfacing of a failure in many patients of a hip implant marketed by DePuy. It would be recalled in 2010. Also in 2010, there was a recall of contact lenses.

Employees had to absorb more bad news in late 2009 when it was announced that 7,500 positions would be eliminated worldwide. Although such "restructurings" are common in most large companies, they have been much less frequent for Johnson & Johnson. (There was a large one in 1998 and a more moderate one in 2004.)

The key to delivering bad news to employees, Jordan says, is to plan everything, from timing to communication vehicles to word choice. Don't sugarcoat it, but give the context. Be sympathetic to those who are losing their jobs and communicate what the company is doing to help them. Expect a downturn in employee engagement from the employees who remain—and then communicate even more faithfully to get engagement back up as soon as possible.

After all, he says, there is a direct link between employee engagement and productivity: "It's intuitive and it's real; studies prove it. So the strategy becomes clear—you must first engage employees."

Corporate Communication, in cooperation with Human Resources, had been measuring employee attitudes and beliefs through a quarterly Pulse survey and a broader biannual Credo survey. It was expected that, because of the 2009 layoffs, favorability ratings of the company by employees would dip, but would soon rebound because employees knew that the restructuring action was rare.

All in all, the picture for J&J as it approached the new decade was "exceptional," Jordan remembers. The effects of patent expirations were being absorbed, and the company was positioning for resumed growth.

And so it was a surprise that, in 2009, J&J learned it had a quality issue with some of its products at McNeil Consumer Healthcare, one of the operating companies in its consumer products division.

The problem that surfaced initially appeared to be a musty odor in certain Tylenol products; the company soon learned that this was due to the leaching of a chemical from the pallets on which boxes of the consumer products were stored.

Other quality issues soon appeared at McNeil, including the finding of minute particles in some medicine during an internal visual inspection.

Ray Jordan: "The company voluntarily recalled as a precaution every unit from any production lot of the pediatric liquid and suspension products manufactured at its Fort Washington, Pennsylvania facility."

Even though the recall was precautionary, it was very broad. So parents found empty shelves where there had been ready inventories of the trusted brand-name medicines for their families. By the end of the year, the company had recalled millions of bottles of products, including Tylenol, Motrin, Benadryl and Zyrtec.

As soon as the crisis began, Jordan was asked to help form and lead a task force comprising business leaders and senior members of the communication, marketing, government affairs, regulatory and legal leadership teams. They met regularly to be sure they were communicating with three strategic objectives in mind: first and foremost, to convey, as broadly and with as much context as possible, news of quality problems as they surfaced; second, to communicate what remediation initiatives were being taken; and, third, to plan and implement a communication program to ultimately restore the brand and corporate reputation.

The interfunctional team looked at looming issues and mapped them in granular detail. Each issue was placed under one of three categories: respond, remediate or restore.

By early 2010, a thorough internal review of manufacturing records and practices at J&J's own manufacturing plants, as well as at all outside suppliers of consumer product materials or ingredients, was well under way. There were departures of senior management in McNeil Consumer Healthcare and the Consumer Products Division. On March 20, 2011, the company announced that it was closing the largest McNeil facility in Fort Washington, Pennsylvania, for major renovations and to ensure that "the manufacturing of our consumer products is restored to the high quality expected of Johnson & Johnson products."

Throughout 2010, J&J communicators candidly acknowledged every consumer-level recall, often personally calling major news media, and double and triple checking to ensure that the news was appropriately disseminated. The recalls soon necessitated a congressional hearing, even though many recalls of faulty medicines that caused much greater risk to health had been immune to such inquiry. After all, this was about Johnson & Johnson, a national treasure . . . and about mothers and infants.

Then-CEO Bill Weldon, testifying before a congressional committee on September 30, 2010: "We recognized then, and we recognize now, that we need to do better, and we will work hard to restore the public's trust and faith in Johnson & Johnson, and strive to ensure that something like this never happens again."

Ray Jordan: "From the day the recalls began in 2009, the employees of J&J were disappointed and embarrassed. People within and outside J&J wanted us to acknowledge the problem and apologize, both of which we did immediately, of course. But they also wanted us to say we had identified the extent of the problem and had fixed it. At that time, we could not say that."

The spotlight shone on Jordan. Observers gave the company high marks for its candor about the quality issues. And no one could dispute that Corporate Communication, working with the senior leadership of J&J, had managed to restrain negative fallout much better than could have been expected given the high level of media attention to the recalls.

All along, the worldwide communication network had continued to support growth of the business, even during what many observers called "turbulent times for J&J." The Corporate Communication team of media, employee and policy communicators, working with investor relations and other divisions, had addressed as best they could questions the recalls raised about causality, impact and implications.

Industry observers and PR pundits said the company should be more transparent and communicative. Why wasn't Jordan talking more? In other words, why wouldn't he say the battle for quality had been won?

Never one to dismiss advice, Jordan was in frequent contact with both internal and external advisors. Many of them pushed for more communication. Consultants who claimed to have "the answer" were constantly trying for his ear.

Going into 2011, most of the pieces were in place for remediation and restoration. Bill Weldon and other members of the executive committee visited scores of plants to verify quality. The supply and quality control operations for the three product segments had been reorganized and centralized.

As J&J senior management gained confidence that the scope of the problem had been defined, the communication strategy could become more aggressive. The media relations people invited top journalists to the New Brunswick headquarters. Corporate Communication began making the CEO and other members of the executive committee available for more interviews.

By mid-2011, some in J&J management were beginning to feel that the first two parts of the communication strategy—acknowledgment and remediation—had worked and that it was time for communication aimed at restoring the equity and corporate reputation. It was time for a major paid institutional advertising campaign.

"It is too early," Ray Jordan told J&J communicators at a May ACCEL course in New Brunswick. "We have to be sure that all the remedial and preventive actions have been taken on the quality control and supply front."

Jordan stood firm. The task force and, ultimately, the executive committee team stood with him.

"We PR folks at J&J," he said, "have always been proud of the work our marketing and advertising colleagues do—from their product ads, to advocating advanced nursing education, to institutional ads about J&J. There will be a need for advertising to help reaffirm the J&J reputation, once remedial and preventive actions have been taken. In the meantime, it's best to keep the media, government and other health-care influentials informed—and allow them to tell the story, arming them with facts and context. In addition, we now have the use of our own unmediated social media channels."

It turned out he was right: it was too early. In late 2011 and into 2012, isolated consumer product recalls occurred that might have gone largely unnoticed in the usual context of health-care products manufacturing. But the media were scrutinizing J&J's every move because of the earlier recalls.

By early 2012, Jordan felt that the time was approaching for the restoration phase of the communication strategy. The Communication Leadership Team had been preparing for a more aggressive campaign to reaffirm the J&J reputation across many fronts. Initial research led them to conclude the following:

- The company has been weathering the storm of recalls, has paid a modest but perceptible reputational price, and is actively pursuing remediation work.
- The views and feelings of some groups—for example, parents—have been affected more than those of others.
- Throughout the crises, J&J employees experienced a greater decline in favorable feelings toward the company than did

other groups. This did not surprise senior management because of the great pride and commitment most employees have.

- Still, the overall favorability rating J&J employees had toward their company—among the highest of companies its size before the recalls—remained high, and had actually moved above its historic highs in recent months.
- Even in this environment, when J&J initiated news coverage, the news reports were more positive than when the company merely reacted.
- Certain groups, J&J investors but others as well, cared about one reputation driver more than any other: the long-term quality of Johnson & Johnson as an investment.

In Chinese, the character that translates into the English word "crisis" means danger plus opportunity. The Tylenol tampering cases of the 1980s resulted in dramatic packaging improvements that not only made Tylenol tamper-resistant and safer for children, but forced other manufacturers to improve their packaging as well.

Ray Jordan in early 2012: "I believe that J&J now faces the 'opportunity' phase of the crisis, and that we will emerge stronger than ever. During the time when we were being besieged with advice to say we had fixed the quality and supply problems, J&J senior management had an advantage: we knew the problems would be overcome and that our consumer products production would be better than ever. Until that day arrived, we had to take our lumps."

The revamped, state-of-the-art McNeil manufacturing facility at Fort Washington, Pennsylvania is scheduled to open by 2014. J&J has stated that it is investing over $100 million in this and other production and quality-control operations.

A crisis usually results in the suspension of business as usual and that, at least for a time, was the case for the J&J communicators in corporate and in parts of the consumer products division. But the communication network had been fortified to the point where it was able to continue to drive increased communication support for business opportunities throughout the balance of the enterprise.

Ray Jordan: "Through both good times and bad our communication group has been focused on moving the ball forward organizationally on a number of fronts."

In a methodical way befitting a man whose education in math, science and business has been real-world tested, Jordan outlines five strategic priorities for public affairs and corporate communication that have transcended good and bad times.

Aligning Communication Leadership: "In 2004, many of our nearly two dozen large businesses at J&J were in need of clearly accountable chief communicators—with internal and external responsibility and a reporting relationship to the senior business leader. As of today, all but one have such a chief communication officer."

Developing Talent: "We are training and motivating J&J communicators to take assignments in different businesses and geographies to advance their careers. The ACCEL program conducted in conjunction with New York University is a trend-setting internal development program that is aligned to this goal."

Improving Analytics: "The communication function is growing consistently more sophisticated in its analytics, having migrated from ad hoc media monitoring to more comprehensive multi-stakeholder reputation assessments that allow for strategic and message planning."

Setting Clear Corporate Narratives: "Communicators have an obligation to help their enterprises be crystal clear on the organization's identity, its character. For us, that means helping to set a clear narrative for our individual companies and the corporation each year. For the enterprise, the narrative is worked out with senior leadership in the fourth quarter; it creates the template for employee, shareholder, investor and media engagements well into the year ahead."

Reaffirming the Credo: "For Johnson & Johnson, our Credo is everything. Communicators work with colleagues in Human Resources to ensure that employees feel they are able to live our Credo, and each year have an opportunity to refresh their own engagement with it."

ON FEBRUARY 21, 2012, THE COMPANY ANNOUNCED THAT ALEX GORSKY, A vice chairman, head of the devices and diagnostics business and a 20-year J&J veteran, would become Johnson & Johnson's new chief executive officer and chairman of the executive committee. He said: "Going forward, our priority is to meet the health and wellness needs of over a billion people a day—and growing. These people and their families all around the world rely on Johnson & Johnson products and services. A big part of our mission involves communication— and our team continues to demonstrate that we are up to the task."

LESSONS

1. The perceptions of an organization held by one group can be vastly different from those held by another. And particular drivers of reputation (for instance, social responsibility, earnings growth, innovation) are more important to certain groups than to others.
2. Organizations that earn it have a reputational halo, but it can be ephemeral and must be earned and re-earned day in and day out.
3. Employee perceptions are often the best indicators of reputational trends.
4. Acknowledge criticism as fair when it is so.
5. Be sure the problem is fixed before credit is taken.

6. Crisis management (a subset of reputation management) is a good thing, but crisis prevention is even better.
7. With every crisis comes an opportunity.
8. Be willing to accept the short-term hit when it is deserved: "Grace under fire."
9. Manage reputation for the long term.
10. Reputation is an asset that must be managed.

PART II

HOW TO PROTECT REPUTATION

SIX

CONTROL THE AGENDA

What Kobe Bryant Knew that Weiner,
Edwards, Clemens, McGwire and Tiger Didn't

BY THE SUMMER OF 2011—AFTER THE US CONGRESS RELUCTANTLY and rancorously raised the debt ceiling, and Standard & Poor's, citing congressional dysfunction, downgraded US debt for the first time in history—the approval of Congress among American voters had plunged to a record low of 9 percent. The other 91 percent thought the Congress was crooked, incompetent or generally the lowest form of human life. (All true!)

Among the reasons were these three men: Charlie Rangel, John Edwards and Anthony Weiner.

All exemplified the very worst kind of arrogance and hubris and presumption of privilege that have helped make Congress one of society's most loathed institutions. (The fact that all three were Democrats was merely coincidence. Republicans also had their share of bad apples. See Delay, Tom; Ney, Bob; and Cunningham, Randy "Duke.")

What Congressman Rangel, former Congressman Weiner and former Senator Edwards also shared was a sense that they could deal with scandal by deflecting and stonewalling as the incriminating reality built against them.

In the end, each learned the hard way that once high-profile institutions or individuals are confronted with scandal, they have two choices: (1) attempt to *control the agenda* or (2) let the agenda control them.

Rangel, Weiner and Edwards, to their eternal detriment, foolishly chose the latter.

THE RISE AND FALL OF CHATTERING CHARLIE

For nearly 40 years, silver-haired, gravelly-voiced Charlie Rangel ruled the roost as one of Washington's most influential and visible Democratic congressmen. The third-longest serving member of the House of Representatives, the loquacious congressman from Harlem was a Korean War veteran, a founding member of the Congressional Black Caucus, the dean of the New York delegation and the chairman of the powerful House Ways and Means Committee.

Rangel was also a go-to guest on all the cable channels, ready to appear whenever the media called—until, that is, he became embroiled in multiple ethics investigations in 2008.

Among the charges: improperly renting four rent-stabilized apartments in his home district, improperly using his office to raise money for the creation of the Rangel Center at the City College of New York, and failing to disclose—and pay taxes on—$75,000 in rental income from his villa in the exclusive Punta Cana section of the Dominican Republic.

Unluckily for Rangel, his primary accuser was his hometown newspaper, the *New York Times*, which ran a series of front-page exposés that painted good ol' Charlie as a larcenous tax cheat and maybe worse.

Rather than confronting the charges and trying to wrestle the agenda from adversarial journalists, Congressman Rangel opted instead to denounce his attackers. Even worse, he chose to do it through an intermediary. And worst of all, his intermediary was a lawyer!

To handle the mounting public firestorm, Rangel called on Lanny Davis, who had earned his spurs defending Bill Clinton against accusations in the Monica Lewinsky affair. When the president ultimately came clean and grimly acknowledged the scope of Ms. Lewinsky's internship activities, lawyer Davis quit the team and got religion.

Specifically, Davis declared himself a "PR man" and wrote a book called *Truth to Tell: Tell It Early, Tell It Yourself*, which generally prescribed what public relations advisors have been counseling for decades: *You might as well tell the truth, because people will find it out eventually.*

Alas, Davis's interpretation of the "truth" as it affected his client Rangel didn't always fit the time-honored prescription he offered in his book. For example:

SELECTIVE DISCLOSURE

Rangel's failure to report his Punta Cana income stretched back two decades. So journalists were naturally curious as to what the congressman had reported over the years.

But Davis refused to part with the congressman's tax returns. Rather, the attorney/PR man offered to provide reporters with paperwork that would show how often the congressman stayed at his exclusive home in the Dominican Republic.

Predictably, offering selective disclosure of the records of a congressman already perceived as slippery only heightened suspicion.

NOT GREEDY, JUST STUPID

A standard chestnut in training clients for media interviews is to ask the victim on camera, "Did you do this because you were *greedy*, or just *ignorant?*" The hoped-for answer, of course, is "neither."

But in Rangel's case, spokes-lawyer Davis was eager to explain away his client's ignorance by saying he was, in fact, *ignorant!*

Davis explained that the congressman—at the time the head of the congressional committee responsible for tax writing—didn't realize he had to declare the rental income. Why not? Well, as Davis explained it, Rangel's wife, Alma, handled the family finances and conferred with their accountant on tax matters.

"This is all news to him," volunteered attorney Davis, not so subtly throwing poor old Alma, Rangel's wife of 42 years who he was in the process of divorcing, under the bus. (A true romantic, he withdrew the divorce petition when she had to file documents specifying his net worth.)

ATTACK THE ATTACKERS

The most difficult public relations advice to deliver to any person in power is *admit you made a mistake.* Powerful people don't like to admit fallibility, even when acknowledging that the truth, as Jesus famously said, "will set you free."

Lawyers, of course, are not Jesus. And even though Chairman Rangel's finances had been under siege for months by the decidedly un-conservative *New York Times,* Davis singled out the paper for "pure newspaper innuendo" and blamed Republicans for "sensationalizing the issue for political gain."

Finally, with a House Ethics Committee hearing looming, Rangel himself tried to win back the agenda with a standing room–only press conference. Admitting his lapse in paying taxes on the property south of the border, Rangel blamed it on "cultural and language barriers."

The beleaguered congressman's belated *"no hablo Español"* defense fell as flat as yesterday's tortillas. In 2010, Rangel was stripped of his committee chairmanship, found guilty of 11 counts of violating House ethics rules, and censured.

Having been spurned by his colleagues and found guilty in the "court of public opinion," the 80-year-old Rangel chose to stubbornly serve out his term in Congress and even consider running for reelection, a pariah to his party and a sad example of refusing to leave the stage even after the curtain has come down.

AN UGLY END FOR A PRETTY-BOY SENATOR

John Edwards had everything as a politician.

The senator from North Carolina was rich, articulate and possessed Brad Pitt-like good looks. Having been his party's candidate for vice president in 2004, he entered the 2008 presidential sweepstakes as a serious contender. The fact that his brave and outspoken wife, Elizabeth, was waging a long, public battle with inoperable breast cancer only added to the Edwards story.

When the despised *National Enquirer* began researching reports of an adulterous affair with a campaign worker in 2007, the Edwards campaign dismissed the rumor. The candidate himself wouldn't dignify the reports by discussing them.

As the presidential primary campaign heated up—and the pressure around Edwards intensified—the candidate continually denied the reported trysts. Smooth as silk, Edwards channeled the million-dollar trial attorney he had once been to parse the facts ever so carefully; to alter, obscure and obfuscate the truth.

For a time, Edwards's slick campaign of dismissal and denial worked. The establishment media shrugged off the *Enquirer* rumors as just another thinly sourced tabloid wild goose chase. But in October 2007, the *Enquirer* lowered the boom, publishing a nailed-down series on how Edwards and campaign videographer Rielle Hunter had carried on an extended affair. To complicate matters even further, the *Enquirer* charged that the two were parents of a love child. So precise were the paper's facts that the mainstream media were left no choice but to pile on.

One might have thought that with the barrage of negative publicity casting him as a liar, Edwards would have bitten the bullet and learned his lesson—that "controlling" this rampaging report was impossible. But no. While the disgraced candidate acknowledged the affair with Hunter in a 2008 ABC News interview, he vehemently denied that he had fathered Hunter's child. The real father of the child, the Edwards camp said, was campaign aide Andrew Young—a "fact" that Edwards's lawyer, Hunter's lawyer, Young's lawyer and even Young himself acknowledged. The only problem was that it was all yet another lie to protect a frantic politician, desperately clinging to his waning power base by enlisting his allies in a grand fabrication.

It is a public relations truism that the *truth will out*. Too-smart-by-half celebrities from Charlie Sheen to Martha Stewart to Bill Clinton have found this out the hard way. And in the cautionary case of John Edwards, the "real truth" is precisely what came out. In short order, all of those around Edwards admitted the lie. The toadying Young, in a humiliating 2010 tell-all memoir, admitted that blind fealty to his charismatic boss caused him to admit siring a child that wasn't his. The child, said Young, was Edwards's, and campaign money had been used to house Hunter and support the off-the-record offspring.

Eventually, in January 2010, way too late to salvage his ruined reputation, Edwards issued a news release admitting that he had fathered Hunter's child. Shortly thereafter, it was reported that the Justice Department was investigating Edwards's use of campaign contributions to hide his affair, and a North Carolina grand jury indicted the former senator on six felony charges, including collecting illegal campaign contributions, conspiracy and making false statements.

John Edwards had missed his chance to come clean, admit his transgressions, tell the truth and win back the agenda. He chose, instead, a path of denial that inevitably led to a 2012 court showdown, where the penalty could be hard time and the choice of cavalierly dismissing the accusations was no longer an option.

WEINER'S WIENER COSTS HIM A SEAT

Where Charlie Rangel *denounced* and John Edwards *dismissed*, Anthony Weiner *deflected* when faced with his own not-so-private purgatory. As was the case with his congressional colleagues, Weiner's attempt to influence the agenda resulted in reputational disaster.

As opposed to his colleague Rangel, who was clearly on the downward skids when scandal broke, and Edwards, whose moment in the sun was about done when his reputation imploded, Anthony Weiner was an up-and-coming Democratic star. A protégé of New York Senator Chuck Schumer, himself the most self-servingly successful publicity seeker this side of Donald Trump, Weiner distinguished himself in 11 years in Congress as one of Washington's most savvy purveyors of public relations.

The combative and charismatic congressman from Brooklyn and Queens was a familiar face on cable TV, even on the dreaded Fox News, where Weiner was a lone liberal willing to mix it up with antagonistic conservative hosts. Weiner gave as good as he got and seemed the odds-on favorite to replace Michael Bloomberg as mayor of New York in 2013.

But Congressman Weiner's talent led to unbridled arrogance which, coupled with his failure to face reality and the unforgiving pervasiveness of the Internet, resulted in a fall from grace that was unprecedented in its velocity.

One day at the end of May 2011, Representative Weiner issued a strange announcement, suggesting that his Twitter account had been hacked and a sexually suggestive photo sent in his name to a young woman in the Northwest. Reporters were intrigued, but when they tried to follow up, the normally effusive congressman was uncharacteristically circumspect. He insisted that his account had been hacked and attempted to deflect the conversation to "issues of much greater importance to our nation."

Representative Weiner evidently failed to understand that to a reporter in the twenty-first century, no issue is of "greater importance" than sex. And despite his repeated attempts to change the subject, not only couldn't Weiner shake the controversy, his curious attempts at deflection served only to attract more journalistic interest. A week after Weiner's hacking announcement, a conservative blogger discovered the truth: Anthony Weiner himself had sent the suggestive photo—in fact a *lot* of suggestive photos—for several years to a healthy list of female Twitter pals. It didn't help matters that the congressman had recently married the well-liked deputy chief of staff and aide to Secretary of State Hillary Clinton.

The day after the blogger's report, Weiner held a raucous press conference, where he admitted everything, acknowledged that he had lied, apologized to his wife and constituents and pledged to "seek help" for whatever it was that was afflicting him. It wasn't enough. Two weeks later, after yet another tweeted photo of Weiner's genitalia was leaked to the press, the congressman announced his resignation and slunk out of public view.

Anthony Weiner's rapid fall from power suggested several reputational lessons for public figures in the twenty-first century:

FIRST, REVIEW "WORST CASE" QUESTIONS BEFORE GOING PUBLIC

The job of the public relations advisor is to make sure that every potentially dangerous or damaging question gets vetted in advance. In the Weiner case, the two most obvious questions were:

1. Did you send the offending tweets?
2. Are the offending photos of you?

What obviously happened was that Weiner and his crew were categorical about the first question and completely ignored the second. They presumably thought that once the congressman had strongly denied sending the tweet, the dialogue would effectively be closed down. They were fatally wrong.

SECOND, EXAMINE THE HIDDEN IMPLICATIONS OF "GOING PUBLIC"

It's also the job of the public relations counselor to scrutinize all the tangential areas that might be exposed once the issue becomes public. In this case, what was *exposed* (besides the obvious), were two curious aspects that added to Weiner's troubles.

1. By insisting that his Twitter account had been hacked, Representative Weiner had an obligation, spelled out in the congressional rulebook, to report the offense to the appropriate authorities. That Weiner refused to do so only made him look more suspicious.
2. In acknowledging the comely coed who was targeted by the offensive tweet, Weiner effectively pointed enquiring reporters to the fact that many of those he followed on Twitter were similarly fetching females.

THIRD, SEX SCANDALS DON'T GO AWAY

Again, if the congressman's brain trust felt that by immediately reporting the "hacking" of Weiner's account, it would swiftly extinguish the controversy—then they simply weren't paying attention. Sex scandals, unlike financial chicanery or other forms of executive malfeasance, stick around for the long term. The roster of contemporary politicians whose good names were soiled by sexual dalliance is legion—along with our friend John Edwards, there are Mark Sanford, Mark Foley, John Ensign, Chris Lee, Gary Hart, Bill Clinton, Barney Frank, Newt Gingrich.

Of all people, Weiner, who made great sport of the suggestive nature of his name, should have known better: when sex is involved, reporters don't let up.

FOURTH, DON'T TWEET

Social media are wonderful but . . . if you're a three-term congressman with easy access to national media and climbing name recognition—for god's sake, don't risk it by using Twitter. It simply ain't worth it.

FIFTH AND FINALLY, CONTROL THE AGENDA

Anthony Weiner prided himself on his sharp tongue and quick mind, which had helped him stay on message and rebut those who tried to knock him off stride. In this case, both his tongue and his mind betrayed him disastrously.

Weiner understood that he couldn't duck the press and that he must stick to his agenda, that is, insist on talking about national issues and not the brewing scandal. Yet his ego got the better of him. At a pivotal moment in his flash crisis, Weiner couldn't resist smacking back when a CNN reporter kept interrupting him at an impromptu street-side press meeting outside the Capitol. Exasperated at the man's incessant badgering, Weiner snapped at the media horde surrounding him, "You do the questions. I do the answers, and this jackass interrupts me. How about that as the new rule of the game?" And with that, he effectively ceded the agenda to an energized press corps that smelled blood and brought him down.

BASEBALL'S STEROIDS HALL OF SHAME

Baseball's "steroids era," the period between 1990 and 2010, when some of the game's brightest stars ingested, injected and otherwise rubbed on illegal anabolic steroids to make them throw harder, run

faster and hit farther, marked the game's lowest point since its nadir in 1919 when members of the infamous Chicago White—i.e.,
Black—Sox threw the World Series.

The poster boys for the steroids era were four of baseball's
brightest stars. Pitcher Roger Clemens and sluggers Mark McGwire,
Sammy Sosa and Barry Bonds were surefire Hall of Famers until
their names and reputations were inextricably linked to performance-enhancing drugs. While all three were revered for much of
their careers, they fell from grace as much from unsuccessful attempts to shift the discussion away from steroids as from taking the
steroids.

Clemens was "the Rocket," a fearsome fire-baller, who threw
smoke and famously refused to allow opposing hitters to get comfortable in the batter's box.

For 13 glorious years, Clemens anchored the Boston Red Sox
pitching corps, winning three Cy Young Awards, the yearly honor
that goes to the league's best pitcher. Then, when the Rocket was
traded by Boston to Toronto at the ripe old age of 35, many (including the Red Sox) thought that Clemens's career was clearly on the
downward slope. But miraculously, in two years in Toronto, Clemens
won the pitching Triple Crown—leading the league in wins, ERAs
and strikeouts—and earned two more Cy Young Awards. From
there, Clemens went on to play another five glorious years for the
New York Yankees, where he won a sixth Cy Young and two World
Series. Next came the Houston Astros, where he won his seventh Cy
Young—more than any other pitcher in baseball history.

All the while, Clemens meticulously honed his professional image. He talked about his intense physical exercise regimen, diet and
work ethic that helped separate him from the other pitchers who
toiled in the game. He played "cat and mouse" on several occasions
with retirement, stimulating intense speculation with each mis-
leading report. The first time Clemens announced his "imminent

retirement" was in 2003. As a result, he enjoyed a well-publicized celebratory "farewell tour" around American League cities. The next year, he "unretired" to pitch for his hometown Astros. And a year later, he signed an $18 million contract—the highest ever for a pitcher—to spend another year with Houston. In 2005, Clemens again implied retirement, only to sign yet again with Houston in 2006 for a $22 million annual contract. In 2007, after Clemens had "absolutely, positively retired," the 45-year-old pitcher unexpectedly showed up in the owner's box at Yankee Stadium and announced he would unretire again to pitch for the Yankees, making a cool $28 million for his effort.

Despite his intense competitiveness, the imposing Clemens was beloved for most of his career. He carefully molded his public relations image to reflect a hard-charging, tough-talking but essentially play-by-the-rules battler. Indeed, with the exceptions of occasionally acting like a diva and one bizarre episode in the 2000 World Series—when a crazed Clemens threw the business end of a sawed-off bat at the Mets' Mike Piazza—the pitcher represented the game with honor. Or so it seemed.

After the 2007 season, when Clemens finally did retire, the conclusion of a report by former Senator George Mitchell was that Roger Clemens, among a host of other ballplayers, was a habitual user of banned anabolic steroids to help his performance. One source of the report was the pitcher's former trainer, who verified that his client regularly injected his buttocks with human growth hormone and other steroids. The outrage from fans and commentators was immediate and unforgiving. Clemens, they concluded, had been "cheating" for years.

The Rocket, used to being in charge of his game and his image, refused to yield. He went on offense, testifying before Congress to firmly deny the steroids allegations; vehemently taking issue with his former trainer on *60 Minutes;* and condemning as hearsay a book written about his use of performance-enhancing drugs. But the steroids story was one issue Clemens couldn't control.

In 2010, a federal grand jury indicted the former pitcher on six felony counts, accusing him of lying before Congress. In the summer of 2011, Clemens's perjury trial began but was suddenly declared a mistrial on the second day of testimony. The government retried the Rocket in 2012, and a jury acquitted him. Clemens had already been declared guilty in the court of public opinion.

MARK MCGWIRE AND SAMMY SOSA—"BIG MAC" AND "SLAMMIN' SAMMY"— were the feel-good story of the summer of 1998, electrifying the baseball world as they matched each other homer for homer on the way toward the revered single-season home-run record, long held by Babe Ruth and then Roger Maris. At season's end, McGwire, the earnest redheaded St. Louis Cardinal, had 70; and Sosa, the happy-go-lucky Dominican Chicago Cub, had 65. And three years later, both were surpassed by Barry Bonds, the rippling, otherworldly San Francisco Giant, who stunned the baseball community with 73 homers in 2001.

But for all three less than a decade later, immortality became ignominy as the performance-enhanced reality of their exploits began to unravel.

Both McGwire and Sosa were prominently mentioned in newspaper reports as among those who tested positive for steroids. As scrutiny increased, both resorted to their own tactics to try to control the agenda. In McGwire's case, he was more than willing to show up at a 2005 congressional hearing about steroids. But when asked directly if he'd ever taken performance-enhancing drugs, the noticeably thinner McGwire not only declined to answer questions directly, but adamantly testified he was there "to look forward not back." His congressional inquisitors, smelling blood, wouldn't let the apoplectic, clearly embarrassed witness off the hook. It was humiliating for

McGwire and uncomfortable to watch. If anyone *looked guilty,* it was the former St. Louis slugger.

At the same congressional hearing, Sosa tried a different tack, feigning language problems (although, in fact, "Slammin' Sammy" spoke English very well). Sosa's attorney spoke for him, stating vigorously that, in his client's words, "I have never injected myself or had anyone inject me with anything. I have not broken the laws of the United States or the laws of the Dominican Republic."

And while the also noticeably thinner Sosa never did acknowledge his steroid use, even attempting an ill-fated comeback attempt, McGwire, five years after his congressional meltdown, finally admitted he had taken performance-enhancing drugs. After signing on as hitting coach with the Cardinals, McGwire decided to "clear the air." In a blubbering interview with Bob Costas, a chastened McGwire claimed that he had only used steroids to recover from injuries and that the use of the drugs had little to do with his heroic exploits on the field. Few were convinced.

And then there was Barry Bonds, the man anyone this side of San Francisco loved to hate. The son of an All Star Giants outfielder, Bonds was another who came into the league a skinny and lithe speedster and miraculously emerged, just a few years later, a bulked-up Adonis. Where McGwire and Sosa were both approachable, Bonds was a sullen and taciturn loner, unloved by both teammates and beat reporters. While his slugging counterparts tried to deflect criticism, when Bonds was accused of "juicing," he simply ignored his accusers and refused to talk about it. When the pressure became too great, he quit baseball. But Bonds's silence and predilection to deny proved his undoing. He was accused of lying to a grand jury convened on the steroids issue and found guilty of obstruction of justice.

The sad fate of Clemens, McGwire, Sosa and Bonds, who went from adulation to vilification in a few short years, could have been avoided. Their use of banned steroids could never be justified, and McGwire's belated attempts to do so only made him look more pathetic. Sosa's feigning of ignorance and Bonds's silence similarly hurt their chances of image redemption. Indeed, in public relations *silence grants the point.* What the four should have done when it became clear that the steroids investigation and findings wouldn't go away was simply tell *the truth.* That's what Roger Clemens's Yankee buddy Andy Pettitte did in 2007 when he, too, was implicated in the steroids scandal. Pettitte admitted that he had used the drugs, apologized and remained a cherished figure in New York. Two years later, another teammate, superstar Alex Rodriguez, used the Pettitte model to acknowledge his steroids use. Rodriguez was applauded for telling the truth and resumed his career.

Both Pettitte and Rodriguez, who relatively quickly came clean about their steroids use, are considered possible Hall of Fame candidates despite having used the banned drugs. Clemens, McGwire, Sosa and Bonds—four undeniably brilliant athletes who refused to confront truthfully the charges leveled against them—will never get in.

IRE OF THE TIGER

Eldrick Tont "Tiger" Woods was well on his way to becoming the greatest, most successful, richest and most idolized golfer in history when it all came crashing down—literally.

In November 2009, when Woods crashed his car outside his Florida home, with his wife reportedly brandishing a golf club "to help get him out," it was a foregone conclusion to everyone but Tiger Woods that *the truth would out.* After he was treated for injuries and released from the hospital, Woods and his entourage went into seclusion, allowing the rumor mill to fill the void. Nature abhors a vacuum, and Tiger Woods's silence set the stage for a tidal wave of news about marital problems, infidelity and "bimbo eruptions" from sea to shining sea; more than a dozen women, in fact, came forward to report extramarital liaisons with the Tiger.

Tiger Woods's immediate seclusion and invisibility helped bury the reputation he and his father and their associates had worked to hone so meticulously over the years. What Woods should have done—what any public figure must do in similar circumstances—was the following:

- First, go public. With TV trucks outside his gated community and paparazzi trying to scale the walls, Woods had little choice but to try to set the agenda early by explaining what had happened. Instead, he chose to adopt a meaningless "Respect our privacy" stoicism. In a crisis, the media "respect" no one's privacy. Indeed, nothing in the world of global icons is "private"—especially when there is the whiff of sex in the air. You've got to go public.
- Second, do it yourself. When companies get in trouble, crisis managers typically advise CEOs to let spokespeople handle the explanation as long as possible. Once the crisis is escalated to the CEO level, you can't throttle it back to a lesser light. On the other hand, some corporate crises—deaths, kidnappings, massive layoffs, etc.—must be handled by the top man or woman, right out of the box. In Woods's case, he couldn't finesse it through a spokesman. Only one person could suitably explain what happened—him.
- Third, get it all out. This is tricky, because the toughest admission for any "master of the universe" is that he or she was *wrong*. But while it was difficult to keep high-profile secrets in the past, today, with the Internet, it's impossible. Woods had no chance to "contain" his infidelities; indeed, millions were downloading images of Tiger's rumored

"hotties" as soon as their names were announced. What Tiger needed to say immediately—but didn't—was that he had "made significant mistakes" and as a result, he and his wife were "going through a rough patch in our marriage, and trying to work it out." Would this have bridled the savage media beasts? No, but in showing immediate courage to face his accusers with the facts, Woods would have been able to salvage, especially among those prone to support him, some goodwill for the fight ahead to win back his reputation.

Sadly, it took Tiger Woods a full three months to begin to control the agenda and finally face the public in a tension-convention "press conference," where no questions were permitted and only friends of the golfer were allowed entry. In a statement delivered with eyes focused on a camera carrying the broadcast live, Woods acknowledged his abhorrent behavior; apologized to his wife, family and fans; and vowed to regain public trust. Certainly, it was too little, too late, but at least it was a start to win back "control" of the agenda and his life.

In subsequent months, Woods tried but failed to regain his supremacy on the golf course. His game, no doubt affected by a long layoff from golf and the stress of the unrelenting media spotlight, had become mortal. He failed to make the cut in a number of tournaments and won no tournaments in 2010, the first time as a professional that he suffered a winless year. Woods fared better, however, on the public relations side. While his marriage had crumbled and his reputation and sponsorships had suffered greatly from the embarrassing escapades revealed by his former lovers, Woods himself seemed more open and willing to face the public. He met with the media more regularly, confronted honestly his inconsistent golf game and remained contrite about his past transgressions.

It remained unclear whether Tiger Woods would ever regain the form that had made him the best golfer in history. Much more certain was the realization that he would never again bask in the pristine reputation he had once enjoyed. But at least in recognizing that in a crisis a public figure can run but can't hide, and in finally confronting with truth the errors of his ways, the tarnished Tiger had begun the long road back to respectability.

BEHAVING REPREHENSIBLY AND EMERGING VICK-TORIOUS

Many obtuse politicians and vainglorious athletes have bitten the dust because they foolishly imagined they could bob and weave their way through a scandal-charred course. There are the few exceptions—stars of politics or sport who got the message, confronted their problems and triumphed in the face of tragedy. Two superstar athletes stand out—having confronted issues far more serious than cheating on their spouses, finagling their taxes or injecting their bodies with banned substances.

Michael Vick and Kobe Bryant played different sports, but both made millions of dollars between the lines and through endorsements. When Vick was accused of cruelty to animals and Bryant was accused of rape, they risked losing not only their livelihoods and freedom but their good names as well. In each case, these athlete icons, charged with heinous crimes, confronted the accusations head on and lived to fight another day.

By 2006, Michael Vick was well on his way to becoming a legend in the National Football League.

The top pick in the NFL's 2001 draft, the southpaw quarterback, who ran faster and threw farther than almost anyone else, had become a three-time all-pro for the Atlanta Falcons. Vick's endorsement income from contracts with Nike, EA Sports, Coca-Cola and other top corporations had earned him 33rd place on Forbes's list of the Top 100 Celebrities in 2005. One magazine reported him as "one of the top 10 richest athletes in the United States."

Vick's problem, like that of many pampered prima donnas at the top of the sports world, was that he felt invincible and above the standards that govern civil society. Vick's problems began in the spring of 2006 when a woman sued him for knowingly giving her herpes. In November, after a disappointing game where he was booed by the hometown Atlanta fans, Vick responded with two well-publicized fingers—a "double-barreled salute," as one reporter labeled it. The quarterback apologized and paid a fine. A few months later, Vick surrendered a water bottle to security at Miami International Airport. The bottle smelled like marijuana and contained a substance in a hidden compartment. The police report characterized the substance as a residue that is "closely associated with marijuana." And even though Vick was later exonerated, he clearly was starting to lose control of his image and, as it turned out, his life.

Later in the year, Michael Vick's troubles escalated exponentially. An investigation by state and federal authorities accused the football star of running an illegal—not to mention, diabolical—dog-fighting complex in Surry County, Virginia. Over the next several months, the depravity of Vick's "Bad Newz Kennels" was displayed for all to see—from the dog-fighting equipment to the 60 pit bulls removed from the complex to the bloody walls and carpets found on the property. Animal lovers and non-animal lovers alike were sickened. In one burst of publicity, Michael Vick had descended from idolized player to ostracized pariah.

Among the indictments faced by Vick and his cohorts was that they "executed approximately eight dogs that did not perform well in 'testing' sessions by various methods, including hanging, drowning, and/or slamming at least one dog's body to the ground." In the twenty-first century, perception is often reality. And before Vick was ever found guilty of these charges, his sponsors, his team and his league didn't wait around, all dropping the quarterback as a spokesman, a player and a member in good standing of the NFL. Bankrupt and alone, Michael Vick was left to fend for himself.

Despite the monstrously bad judgment he had demonstrated in getting into this mess, Michael Vick's instinct as to how to get out of it was simple genius. After debating briefly whether to fight the allegations, Vick changed fields, faced up and fessed up to his guilt. He accepted a plea agreement from the federal government along with jail time for what he had done. And a humbled, dark-suited Michael Vick, without a script or an advisor alongside him, told a jammed press conference and a national TV audience, "Dog fighting is a terrible thing. I reject it." He vowed to redeem his reputation and return to football, and then headed to Leavenworth, Kansas, for 23 months in prison.

Vick's simple actions of accepting jail time, acknowledging his crime and facing the media and the public to answer all outstanding questions effectively seized control of the agenda and allowed the player to become master of his own fate. Had he fought the charges and refused to face his accusers, Vick would only have exacerbated the opprobrium directed at him and made any attempt at a comeback that much harder.

As soon as he was released from prison at the still-young age of 30, Vick used the goodwill he had begun to build by agreeing to fight against animal abuse, even appearing before Congress to testify in favor of the Animal Fighting Spectator Prohibition Act of 2011. The NFL, convinced that the player had learned his lesson and paid his debt to society, reinstated him, and Vick quickly regained his form as the quarterback of the Philadelphia Eagles.

As final proof of the correctness of Vick's decision to earn back control of his agenda, in 2011 Nike officially re-signed him—the first time a sponsor had ever brought back an athlete it had dropped.

Oh yes, and in August of that year, the once-bankrupt, seemingly washed-up quarterback signed a six-year contract extension with the Eagles for a cool $100 million.

STRATEGICALLY SAVING THE BRYANT BRAND

As well as Michael Vick handled his brush with infamy, few celebrities in modern-day history have so convincingly come back from near image destruction as Kobe Bryant.

Bryant, the Los Angeles Lakers perpetual all-star, was arguably the best player in the National Basketball Association. The scion of a well-respected NBA family, Bryant was a golden boy—a good-looking, hardworking and seemingly devoted husband and father, who faithfully smooched his little daughters on the way to the locker room after each victory. And Bryant honed his image scrupulously—carefully guarding his public statements, remaining aloof and keeping his private life private. Like baseball's circumspect superstar Derek Jeter, Kobe Bryant was a marketer's dream. By 2003, in fact, Bryant had lucrative endorsement deals with a host of A-list companies from McDonald's to Coca-Cola and had signed a deal to create a line of Nike signature sneakers for a cool $45 million.

But that June, disaster struck Kobe Bryant's near-perfect world. After staying at a Colorado spa lodge in advance of undergoing knee surgery, Bryant was named as a suspect in an investigation by the Eagle, Colorado sheriff's office. A 19-year-old hotel employee accused the NBA star of rape. Bryant, she said, ordered room service, and when she delivered it, he sexually assaulted her. The news sent shock waves across the country and battered Bryant's erstwhile bulletproof reputation. Within weeks, McDonald's and other sponsors dropped Bryant from their endorsement roster, and sales of his replica jersey—which had led all other NBA players'—fell precipitously. Nike, one of the brashest and most outspoken corporations in America, was uncharacteristically silent about the calamity that had befallen its most visible spokesman.

In July, the other shoe dropped; the Eagle County district attorney formally charged the Lakers star with one count of felony sexual assault. If Bryant was convicted, the charges would carry a prison term of four years to life, and his reign as the darling of professional basketball, not to mention his dominance as a paid endorser, would be toast.

Faced with the most egregious of criminal charges, abandoned by most of his sponsors and caught in a bottomless pit of scurrilous rumors and innuendo, Kobe Bryant resorted to a most unorthodox public relations strategy: he seized control of his own agenda.

Less than four hours after the Eagle DA's announcement, a composed and somber Bryant convened his own press conference at the Los Angeles Staples Center to proclaim his innocence. With his wife at his side, Bryant acknowledged having extramarital sex with his accuser, but he insisted it was "consensual."

Clutching his wife's hand, an alternately terse and tearful Bryant said, "I didn't force her to do anything against her will. I'm innocent. I sit here in front of you guys, furious at myself, disgusted at myself for making the mistake of adultery. And I love my wife with all my heart . . . I'm innocent. And together my wife and I and our family, we're going to fight these false accusations."

Bryant's performance, while excruciating to watch, was nonetheless masterful in not only presenting another explanation for what had happened, but also in personalizing and humanizing a suspected rapist, recently portrayed as a cold and arrogant brute. In single-handedly confronting the damning allegations and facing up to a skeptical press corps, Bryant was perceived as earnest, candid and even brave. Most important, Bryant's press conference succeeded in wresting back control of his rapidly spiraling disaster.

It was a miraculous performance, as virtuoso as any he had accomplished on the basketball court. And it instantly changed the dynamics of the perceived case against him and put his accuser squarely on the defensive.

From the moment he left the stage at the turning-point press conference, Kobe Bryant said little else about the case in Colorado. He returned to the court, kept his focus on basketball and allowed his lawyers to take over the details of extricating him from a suicidal situation. In time, Bryant's accuser—herself now the subject of damaging stories in the press as to motives and background—decided she couldn't stomach a trial, and the Eagle County prosecutor dropped the case. In March 2005, two years after the ugliness began, Bryant and the woman settled a civil lawsuit filed against him, with terms kept private. Kobe Bryant was once again free to build back his career and reputation.

A year later, Bryant scored 81 points in a single game. A year after that, he was named the league's Most Valuable Player, and the next year he led the Lakers to the league championship. Meanwhile, the player who many experts predicted would permanently lose his marketing luster gradually regained his position at the top of the endorsement ladder. Nike, silent for the two years that Bryant's fate remained unclear, launched a new line of shoes in his name. Even Coca-Cola, which had dropped the star like a hot croissant when he got in trouble, hired him to promote its Vitaminwater brand.

Kobe Bryant's bold decision to take action, lay out his view of events and open himself to public scrutiny had rescued his career, his future and his reputation. And whether or not one ultimately believed his version of events, Bryant's unprecedented public relations action set a new standard in taking back an agenda that, if allowed to persist unchallenged, could have proven fatal to his income, his image, his good name and his freedom.

THE BRYANT PRINCIPLE

What can we deduce from this rogues' gallery of politicians and athletes? Several things.

Charlie Rangel finagled his taxes and tried to deflect. Anthony Weiner texted his privates and tried to deny. John Edwards betrayed his wife and tried to dismiss. Tiger Woods did likewise and tried to disappear. And Roger Clemens, Mark McGwire, Sammy Sosa and Barry Bonds bent the rules and tried to walk away unscathed. All ended with their reputations shredded and their lives in ruin.

By contrast, when faced with an even more scandalous accusation—brutally abusing animals—Michael Vick chose the difficult path of confirming the allegations, acknowledging his trespasses and vowing to chart a new course toward redemption. Vick realized early on in his crisis that attempting to "whistle past the graveyard" was an impossible option, particularly for an individual in the public eye. So he went public and took charge of his agenda and his destiny.

The point is that it is, indeed, painful for someone—particularly a public someone—to admit that he or she done wrong. But it is necessary to clear the air in order to salvage any hope of regaining one's own agenda. Indeed, it is axiomatic in public relations—especially in a modern world of TMZ.com and tweets and Facebook postings and blogs and cable TV and talk radio—that *the best offense is a truthful defense.* That is, in the twenty-first century, one can only regain the high ground after admitting the truth, apologizing for past behavior, vowing to learn from mistakes, and then personifying, through improved action, a changed and chastened individual.

This public relations axiom might as well be labeled the Bryant Principle after the twenty-first-century superstar who used it so decisively to win back his earning power and earn back his reputation.

LESSONS

1. Never deflect.
2. Never dismiss.
3. Never denounce.
4. Silence grants the point.
5. The best offense is a truthful defense.
6. People will often forgive even a major misstep if the apology is swift, complete and unqualified.
7. The greater the sexual content, the greater the chance for major scandal.
8. Tweet at your peril.
9. To win the day, control the agenda.
10. The best advice is to do the right thing.

SEVEN

TAKE EITHER ROAD— JUST STICK TO IT

How Hewlett-Packard Went High,
Dominique Strauss-Kahn Went Low,
and They Both Won

IT IS HUMAN NATURE THAT AS ONE GETS OLDER, LIKE YOUR AU-
thors, he or she becomes more crotchety, pining for the "good old
days" and lamenting the degradation of modern society. But crotchety or not, most would agree that in the twenty-first century, standards—in literature and language, media and politics, and a great
many other areas—have taken a beating. In all aspects of modern
life, civil discourse, calm communication and reasoned compromise
have taken a back seat to bellicosity, browbeating and an attitude of
"my way or the highway."

It shouldn't be this way, but as Walter Cronkite used to say,
"That's the way it is." In the old days (before Twitter, Facebook,
blogs, cable "news" and talk radio), more often than not, it was the

reasonable and rational and honorable argument that triumphed in the court of public opinion. Today, not so much. Too often in the modern world, it's the arrogant or boastful or belligerent who win recognition and gain credibility. How else to explain Donald Trump or Al Sharpton or Nancy Grace?

Whereas the major newspapers and TV networks once provided editorial filters for what constituted news, today's media are more Wild West. The Internet is an unedited free-for-all, with self-serving, credentially challenged bloggers and tweeters capriciously conveying rumor and gossip and hunches as "fact." Meanwhile, mainstream media, concerned about missing a *real* story, increasingly reprise such undocumented Net nuggets, thereby giving them credence and "legs." This vicious cycle occasionally results in fiction being portrayed as fact, in pretenders being promoted as professionals.

Now what effect does all this have on one's reputation and public image in the twenty-first century? Plenty. In the old days, when journalistic standards were higher, you could pretty well count on phonies being found out and the truth prevailing. It made sense, therefore, for companies and individuals to take the "high road" in any dispute or controversy, adopting a strategy of maintaining decorum and letting the facts speak for themselves, trusting that society would assess the outcome in a reasonable, rational way. But today, with standards lowered and pack-mentality journalism the rule rather than the exception, the high road may not always be the best one. Sometimes, it is the "low road"—adopting a strategy based on opposition research, rumors and innuendo to besmirch an adversary—that leads to success.

The "road" one chooses depends on the facts of the case, the adversary on the other side and the inherent integrity of the organization or individual. Two recent examples—Hewlett-Packard's firing of popular CEO Mark Hurd in 2010 and the dismissal of sexual assault charges against former International Monetary Fund managing director Dominique Strauss-Kahn in 2011—illustrate how either the high road or the low road can result in victory.

HOW HP TOOK THE HIGH ROAD AND FIRED ITS POPULAR CHIEF

As difficult as it may be to believe, given all the disastrous twenty-first-century decisions of the company's board and management, Hewlett-Packard was once a legendary Silicon Valley colossus.

Its founders, Bill Hewlett and David Packard—Stanford classmates who in 1939 started with an audio oscillator in a garage and went on to build the world's largest information technology company, the first with revenues in excess of $100 billion—were highly ethical individuals.

Both Hewlett and Packard, after they retired, became well known as philanthropists, each of them the epitome of high ethics and propriety.

The hugely successful company they developed was built on a platform of innovative competence complemented by an understated public profile and high moral fiber. Then HP stunned the macho high-tech world in 1999 by recruiting an actual *woman* to be its CEO. Carly Fiorina, high-profile executive vice president of AT&T, was the surprise selection to take the Hewlett-Packard reins, becoming one of the most powerful women in business.

Before long, everything unravelled. Fiorina's tenure was marked by a contentious merger with rival computer maker Compaq, dissension in the ranks, and a most un-HP-like parade of personal CEO publicity. "Carly Mania" reigned in the media. Publicity about HP's woman chief, unlike the case with her more muted predecessors, seemed to be all over the place. In 2005, having had enough fireworks, the Hewlett-Packard board ushered CEO Fiorina out the door. And five years later, the former HP CEO ran unsuccessfully in California for the U.S. Senate.

As Fiorina's permanent replacement, Hewlett-Packard chose Mark Hurd, a no-nonsense, 25-year computer industry veteran who had headed NCR Corporation. Hurd's background at NCR covered all areas of the company. His reputation was impeccable. At Hewlett-Packard, unlike his predecessor, Hurd proved himself a solid, low-key leader, well respected by Wall Street and the media, if not always by the people who worked for him. (He laid off 10 percent of the HP workforce shortly after being named CEO.) Hurd generally managed the company skillfully, regaining much of the credibility it had sacrificed in the Fiorina era. The new CEO did, however, have to withstand one *doozy* of a crisis along the way.

SPYING ON ITSELF

In September 2006, *Newsweek* published a cover story revealing that the chairwoman of Hewlett-Packard's historically dysfunctional board of directors, Patricia Dunn, had hired a team of independent electronic-security experts to spy on fellow HP board members, staff members and journalists who covered the company.

Dunn was concerned about "persistent disclosure of confidential information from within the ranks." The primary target of the investigation was the company's longest-serving board member, George A. Keyworth II, a notoriously loose-lipped physicist and former presidential science advisor, who had earlier been asked to resign but refused.

To "get the goods" on its board members, the HP electronic-security experts used a technique known as "pretexting" to obtain call records of board members and nine journalists, including reporters for CNET, the *New York Times* and the *Wall Street Journal.* The investigators misrepresented themselves to phone companies as board members and journalists in order to obtain phone records.

When the spying was revealed, a reeling Chairwoman Dunn claimed she hadn't known which methods the investigators planned to use to determine the source of the leaks. Later, it came out that Dunn was briefed regularly on the findings of the investigation, including the source of leaks and the techniques used to get information.

The revelations of ethical impropriety from one of the nation's historically most ethical companies sent reverberations throughout the business community.

- The California attorney general charged Dunn with four felonies for her role in the HP investigation into the unauthorized disclosure of company information. (The charges were dropped a year later "in the interest of justice.")
- The Securities and Exchange Commission launched a full-scale investigation. Lawsuits were filed. HP's stock price tumbled.
- Congress leaped into the fray with hearings. And journalists kept exposing new elements of HP's spying.

Just weeks after the first stories appeared, Hurd, who had kept a low profile during the scandal, announced that Dunn had resigned; he apologized profusely for HP's violation of the privacy of directors and company employees. Not only did Hurd escape the board crisis relatively unscathed, he was named to succeed Dunn as HP chairman.

"A CLOSE PERSONAL RELATIONSHIP"

For five years, Hurd navigated Hewlett-Packard through steadily better years; the company appeared to be back on its profitable and ethical track. That's why it was such a bolt from the blue on Friday, August 6, 2010, when it was announced that CEO Hurd had decided to resign.

According to HP's board, which made the announcement after the market closed, CEO Hurd resigned, technically, for "fudging on his expenses." Less technically, but more importantly, Hurd was found to be having a two-year "close personal relationship" with a female contractor. Part of Hurd's "relationship" with the contractor included dinners, often on business trips, for which the CEO charged the company but failed to report that he had dined with his friend, the contractor.

And so, because of these, ahem, "expense irregularities," the HP board fired the CEO. Not incidentally, the "contractor" in question happened to be a blond bombshell and former aspiring B-movie actress turned seminar leader, featured in such stellar cinematic properties as *Intimate Obsession, Blood Dolls* and the immortal *Body of Influence 2*. As soon as the "contractor" was implicated in the HP scandal, she retained notorious show biz lawyer and publicity-seeking missile Gloria Allred to file a sexual harassment suit against Hurd.

ATTRACTING THE WRATH OF THE CHATTERING CLASS

In making its announcement about its well-regarded CEO, HP went to great lengths to acknowledge that after an extensive investigation, it found that Hurd had committed no violations of law but had violated the Hewlett-Packard Code of Conduct. So the board had "no recourse" but to ask for and receive Hurd's resignation.

Hurd himself was candid in admitting that he had not always represented the corporation in the manner in which he should have. He said, "I realized there were instances in which I did not live up to the standards and principles of trust, respect and integrity that I have espoused at HP and which have guided me throughout my career . . . I believe it would be difficult for me to continue as an effective leader at HP and I believe this is the only decision the board and I could make at this time."

The HP board, also to its credit, acknowledged that offing such a well-respected leader was a difficult decision. Said its lead independent director, "The board deliberated extensively on this matter. It recognizes the considerable value that Mark has contributed to HP over the past five years in establishing us as a leader in the industry. . . . This departure was not related in any way to the company's operational performance or financial condition, both of which remain strong. The board recognizes that this change in leadership is unexpected news for everyone associated with HP."

So why get rid of him, then? That's what HP's critics—and they were legion—wanted to know. Many, in fact, were only too ready to denounce Hewlett-Packard publicly for adopting such a hard line relative to a clearly productive CEO.

First out of the box was Larry Ellison, billionaire co-founder of software giant Oracle, a tennis buddy of Hurd's and a man rarely cited for modesty, probity or virtue. In typical understatement, Ellison declared, "The HP Board just made the worst personnel decision since the idiots on the Apple Board fired Steve Jobs many years ago," adding that the HP board capitulated to "cowardly corporate political correctness."

The comparison with the Jobs firing, of course, was oranges-to-apples. Jobs left Apple the first time in the mid-1980s because of an industry sales slump, declining Apple revenues and personality differences with others in management. Hurd, by contrast, left because he had violated corporate policy having nothing to do with operations or sales. As far as Oracle's Ellison was concerned, corporate conduct policy or not, Hurd was a good CEO; therefore, the Ellison reasoning went, the company should have sacrificed its principles and retained him.

Corporate governance watchdog Nell Minow took the board to task for failing "to make it clear enough to [Hurd] what their expectations were or this would not have happened." After all, Minow argued, the board is responsible for "making sure the CEO knows he will be held accountable."

Minow's argument seemed to rest on the presumption that an executive as high powered as the CEO shouldn't be expected—as every other employee is—to actually *read* the Code of Conduct. According to her, it is apparently the board's responsibility to explain how the code applies to the CEO, as if the head man or woman should be subject to different standards than the rest of the company. This argument, on its face, was as specious as Ellison's. Clearly, the CEO should be subject to the same rules that govern other employees. That was the principle on which the Hewlett-Packard board took a stand. And its members should have been applauded for it, especially by a self-described "corporate governance watchdog."

Finally, there were the industry analysts in the financial community and the press who joined in to pile on HP for getting rid of such a market-friendly CEO.

The tech analyst at Sanford C. Bernstein and Co. said it was "difficult to view Hurd's departure as anything but negative for HP." Likewise, argued *e-Week,* a leading IT management journal, "The goal of any major tech company is to maximize shareholder value. The only way to do that is to reduce expenses, increase revenues and ultimately see profits soar. When a CEO who has done as good a job as Hurd leaves, shareholders tend to get worried. And when that happens, they usually start selling off shares for fear of the next CEO ruining things."

Which is, of course, what happened immediately after Hurd's departure from HP: its shares tumbled. But investors realized—even if industry analysts didn't—that a successful company that actually *stands for something* is a good investment in the long run. Accordingly, HP shares soon regained the value they had lost.

STICKING TO HIGH-ROAD PRINCIPLE

Hewlett-Packard's critics had a point. The company's board did have at least two other options, both employed time and again by organizations facing similar crises.

One, it could have looked the other way, quietly slapped the CEO on the wrist and hoped nothing would be made public.

This is the road taken by many more timid companies in similar circumstances. It mollifies Wall Street and the stockholders, sacrificing principle for performance. But such a response sends a nasty message to employees that management is different, more entitled than rank-and-file workers and, therefore, held to a lower standard in terms of ethics and propriety. It's the wrong message, and over time, it destroys a company's credibility—particularly with the people who work for it, but with its shareholders as well.

Two, HP could have announced Hurd's resignation to "pursue personal business opportunities" and offered no further explanation.

This, too, is a road taken by many organizations, who'd rather keep the messy divorce details out of the public dialogue. Bank of America once famously made such an announcement regarding the sudden, premature departure of the CEO's heir apparent. The announcement was so suspect on its face, and B of A's handling of it so ham-handed, that ultimately the FBI investigated, and a grand jury was impaneled to get to the bottom of the situation. (The real story was that the heir apparent violated the Bank of America Code of Conduct and was asked to leave.)

No, what Hewlett-Packard did in the Hurd case was laudable and correct. Its action reinforced that the company's Code of Conduct wasn't just a piece of paper that meant nothing; by contrast, it represented a mandatory pact to which every employee, regardless of rank, was subject. In taking strong action against the highest-ranking individual in the company, HP's board remained true to the ethical framework established by its founders and demonstrated the three-step template to which all companies should adhere in a similar management crisis.

First, perform properly.

In this case, Hewlett-Packard created a Code of Conduct that dictated employee performance standards. Every HP employee, from those in the mailroom to those in the CEO's office, was expected to adhere to the requirements and be subject to the sanctions of that code. CEO Hurd violated the code, and he was dealt with accordingly.

The true test of the meaningfulness of the HP Code of Conduct—and the measure of what Hewlett-Packard stands for—were on trial in the Mark Hurd case. By finding the CEO guilty of violating the code, HP stayed true to its principles—i.e., *no matter the rank, no one is above the law*—and burnished its reputation.

Second, the behavior must match the performance.

Okay, Mark Hurd violated the Code of Conduct. "But why fire the guy?" asked Larry Ellison. Here's why.

The CEO sets the tone for the corporation. Ergo, he or she must be held to an even *higher standard* with respect to such violations as conflict of interest, falsifying expenses or using corporate resources for personal interest. HP could easily have, as Hurd's friend Ellison intimated, slapped the CEO on the wrist, fined him, warned him, reduced his bonus, etc. But leadership organizations—which Hewlett-Packard has always been—don't cop out like that. They stand up for what they stand for. And when someone in the organization defies the very ethical principles upon which the company is based, a leadership company will respond accordingly.

In the Hurd case, a CEO acting cavalierly with the shareholders' resources was a *serious* matter that needed to be dealt with seriously. The Hewlett-Packard board behaved precisely in the manner mandated by the CEO's infraction. In so doing, the board sent a clear and unmistakable message to all current and future HP employees who might question the importance of the Code of Conduct.

Third, get the facts out to tamp down aftershocks.

Hewlett-Packard was smart to lay out the facts as to why the board pushed Hurd out, rather than pretending the CEO really left on his own accord. In so doing, they limited the inevitable fallout from such a bolt-from-the-blue story.

The official announcement answered most of the outstanding questions in terms of (1) the CEO's questionable relationship with a contractor, (2) the nature of the investigation of Hurd's activities that the board had ordered, (3) the conclusion that there was no evidence of sexual harassment, but that (4) the CEO clearly had violated HP's Standards of Business Conduct. The announcement praised the outgoing CEO for his operational accomplishments, quoted him as acknowledging that he had erred and reassured the world that the HP bench was deep and competent. In other words, the official announcement achieved exactly what it takes to short-circuit a brewing crisis:

- It preempted most questions that the announcement might engender.
- It accepted board responsibility for the decision and spelled out clearly why it did what it did and why the punishment was right.

While reasonable observers might disagree with aspects of the HP decision and response, they can't quibble about the fact that the Hewlett-Packard board displayed admirable courage in taking a clearly unpopular action in order to safeguard the principles upon which the company was built. The board took the high road and distinguished itself.

Sadly for Hewlett-Packard's board, its moment of leadership glory was short-lived. To replace Hurd as CEO, the board chose Léo Apotheker, the failed former CEO of German software giant SAP, which curiously refused to renew Apotheker's contract after he spent only seven months on the job. The apparent reason for SAP's reluctance to retain its former top man became more obvious after Apotheker miserably bungled his first several months at the helm of Hewlett-Packard. For one thing, he made the monumental mistake of producing a product to compete head to head with Apple's untouchable iPad. HP ignominiously dropped the product after only 48 days of meager sales. For another, he suggested that HP might abandon its pivotal PC division. And then, in 2011, Apotheker announced that HP would buy British software maker Autonomy for a whopping $10 billion in cash, a price that made securities analysts blanch. Accordingly, HP's stock sank like a stone.

Not unsurprisingly, in the fall of 2011, the Hewlett-Packard board threw Apotheker over the side after only 11 months of his "leadership." (At least they bit the bullet quickly.) To replace Apotheker, the HP board chose Meg Whitman, former CEO of eBay, who had most recently flopped as a 2010 candidate for governor of California after spending $174 million of her own money to lose the race.

With its disastrous decision to hire Léo Apotheker and its embarrassment in firing him within a year of his appointment, the Hewlett-Packard board was assailed once again by the naysayers for its "first wrong decision to fire Mark Hurd." To add insult to injury, former HP CEO Hurd was doing just fine, having been hired by (who else?) Larry Ellison as co-president and board member of Oracle Corporation.

"Our reputation and our success depend upon the personal commitment that each of us makes to uphold our values and practice ethical behavior in all of our business dealings. All of us, regardless of employment level, position, or geographic location, are expected to make this commitment daily, both individually and collectively, to uphold the standards of business conduct outlined in this Code."

Thus, ironically, spoke Lawrence J. Ellison in the preamble to Oracle Corporation's Code of Conduct; words, no doubt, that the public relations tone-deaf CEO passed along to his new co-president.

NO LONGER "NO" TO GOING LOW

For anyone with a conscience, a sense of morality, or a belief in a higher purpose—beyond making money or grabbing power—taking the public relations high road is always preferable. People and institutions make wrong decisions and commit errors. It's inevitable. Nobody is perfect. And nine times out of ten, the best public relations advice is to tell the truth and suffer the consequences. Indeed, no self-respecting public relations counselor would ever instruct his or her client to *lie*.

But on the other hand . . . in this age of declining societal standards, where millions take at face value what they read on an undocumented Internet blog and where opinionated loudmouths inspire legions of lemmings who believe every word . . . taking the low road can pay off for the right kind of character. For example:

Nancy Grace, a former Georgia prosecutor once described by an appeals court as playing "fast and loose" with the facts, has used that very "attribute" to become a twenty-first-century TV star.

Grace first came to media attention by using the murder of her college fiancé as a rallying cry to seek truth and justice. It was later revealed that Grace's "recollections" of the facts of that case were a bit off. Among them, her fiancé was killed by a coworker, not a random stranger, as Grace had said repeatedly; the coworker had no criminal record and admitted to the crime, contrary to how Grace characterized him; and he filed no appeals after conviction, again contrary to Grace's story.

Grace's rabid, devil-eye style, first on the then-fledgling Court TV, then on more rational CNN and finally on the over-the-top HLN (Headline News) has made mincemeat of America's time-honored "guilty till proven innocent" standard. Grace's one-woman judge and jury routine has, among other travesties of justice:

- Claimed unequivocally that a drifter suspected in the Utah kidnapping of a teenager in 2002 "was guilty." The drifter died in custody and later was posthumously exonerated when two other individuals confessed to the crime.
- Accused members of the 2006 Duke lacrosse team of "gang raping" a stripper. The more it became clear that the young men were innocent, the more she used her bully TV pulpit to persecute them.
- Badgered unmercifully the mother of a missing two-year-old. The day the interview was scheduled to air, the woman killed herself. Relatives blamed her death on Grace's over-the-top interview and sued. Grace settled with the woman's estate.

In an earlier, more rational time, crazed broadcasters were chastised, suspended and ultimately replaced if they refused to honor the truth or propriety. But in the twenty-first century, outrage and righteous indignation, rather than truth and accuracy, are what lead to higher network profits. And so not only were Nancy Grace and her employers unrepentant for the verbal damage she had wrought, she—and they—reveled and prospered in the low-road notoriety.

She was even drafted to appear on *Law and Order* and chosen to compete on *Dancing with the Stars,* where she embarrassingly exposed a nipple in a particularly vigorous quickstep. Grace, typically, was unfazed. (Tough to imagine Walter Cronkite in a similar predicament.)

Unlike prosecutor Grace, Al Sharpton gained his notoriety on the other side of the defense table. Sharpton's prominence as a civil rights activist came primarily from his orchestrated campaign of race-baiting rabble-rousing in and around New York City that landed him regularly on the front page of the city's tabloids and just as often in the slammer.

But just as Nancy Grace's crusade to win fame through outrageous views did, indeed, get her noticed, so too did Sharpton's low-road tactics of blatant publicity seeking, regardless of the truth, parlay him into the national spotlight.

Sharpton's most infamous abrogation of decency was his nonstop verbalizing in the case of a troubled 15-year-old African American girl, Tawana Brawley, who claimed in 1987 that she had been assaulted and raped by six white men. Sharpton vilified the prosecutor in the case and accused him not only of racism but of being one of the girl's attackers. After Brawley acknowledged she had made the whole thing up and Sharpton was found guilty of slandering the prosecutor and sentenced to pay a fine, Rev. Al went silent and refused to ante up, leaving the fine to be paid by friends.

Despite an arguably questionable record with no shortage of controversy, Sharpton just kept talking. And boy could he talk—argumentatively, accusingly, defiantly. And an unchallenging media couldn't get enough of him. From the distinguished *Meet the Press* to the fearsome Fox News Rasputin Bill O'Reilly, nobody could lay a glove on Reverend Al. And few challenged him. Indeed, it was the largely unquestioning media that anointed Sharpton with his otherwise inexplicable credibility.

And despite a career that could charitably be described as *check-ered,* Al Sharpton ascended to the point where he not only ran for the 2004 Democratic presidential nomination and was awarded his own MSNBC talk show in 2011, but his approval was even courted by a sitting president! In 2011, Barack Obama paid a special visit to Rev. Al to seek his reelection support. And in 2012, the most pow-erful lawyer in the land, President Obama's Attorney General, Eric Holder, made a pilgrimage to Rev. Al's National Action Network an-nual meeting in Washington. As Yogi Berra once said when they told him the citizens of Dublin had just elected a Jewish mayor, "Only in America."

Perhaps the greatest example of how pursuing the low road can result in twenty-first-century fame and fortune is the saga of Donald Trump. "The Donald"—although you'd never know it from hearing the real estate baron's self-aggrandizing claims—is the quintessential "born on third base" American success story. Trump's father Fred was a careful, cagey real estate developer who owned city blocks full of multistory Brooklyn, Queens and Staten Island apartment buildings, populated by 27,000 upstanding, rent-paying residents. Best of all, Fred Trump's residential real estate empire was virtually debt free.

By the time of his death in 1999, Fred Trump had amassed a $400 million estate, which he left largely to his children. Thus was born the "grassroots" success saga of America's most obnoxious, self-promoting salesman since P. T. Barnum.

Donald Trump's business career began while he was a student at the Wharton Business School, in his father's office at the Elizabeth Trump & Son real estate company. After he took control of the com-pany, young Donald quickly made clear how he planned to "share" power and recognition by wiping his grandmother's name from the masthead and renaming the firm The Trump Organization.

Capitalizing on what his father had left him, Donald Trump's own business successes were notable, among them developing apartment complexes on the West Side of Manhattan, building New York's Grand Hyatt Hotel, and restoring the Wolman Skating Rink in Central Park. But just as notable—although Trump didn't like to acknowledge them—were a series of business clunkers. At the height of New York's real estate recession in the 1990s, when both his Trump Plaza Hotel and New Jersey's Taj Mahal casino went bust, Trump was brought to the brink of personal bankruptcy. Had it not been for the city's commercial banks cutting him slack (due largely to the debt-free Fred Trump empire he would soon inherit), the twenty-first-century story of the bombastic builder might have been far different.

But Donald Trump sold off properties like the Trump Shuttle airline and lucrative Manhattan real estate to escape the clutches of the banks and reemerged in the boom years of the new century, bent on seizing every opportunity to reinforce his status as a legend in his own mind.

Never in doubt and always quotable, Donald Trump proved a darling of the twenty-first-century media, more interested in style than substance. Indeed, few were more successful than Trump in converting his many marriages, quick-trigger lawsuits (directed especially at those who questioned his success and net worth), frequent bullying and constant bragging into book deals, TV shows and recurring flirtations with running for president on the Republican side.

One could only imagine a day when the fate of the republic would lie in a choice for the highest office in the land between Al Sharpton and Donald Trump. At least Nancy Grace hasn't threatened to run for president—yet!

The point is that, in the twenty-first century, as these three egotistical, singularly-focused individuals have illustrated, the heretofore contemptible course of building a reputation through pursuing the *low road* can no longer be dismissed. On the contrary, as the bizarre case of one of the world's highest-ranking financiers suggests, the low road may sometimes be the only road to escape reputational ruin.

IMF CHIEF TAKES THE LOW ROAD AND ESCAPES SEXUAL ASSAULT CHARGES

In the spring of 2011, few international financial figures were more powerful than Dominique Strauss-Kahn, managing director of the International Monetary Fund. The dashing 62-year-old Frenchman, who ruled the IMF with a strong and confident hand, lived in the Georgetown section of Washington, DC, with his third wife, the French journalist and art heiress Anne Sinclair. Many believed Strauss-Kahn was on course to become the next president of France.

But a not-so-funny thing happened to the aristocratic "DSK," as he was known, on his way to the presidency. His trip was derailed by a housekeeper at New York City's Sofitel Hotel who accused the IMF bigwig of sexually assaulting her on his way out the door.

Strauss-Kahn, about to get on a plane back to France, was intercepted at JFK airport by agents of the Manhattan district attorney's office and promptly arrested, sending shockwaves across financial capitals around the world.

Strauss-Kahn, according to spanking new Manhattan DA Cyrus R. Vance Jr., son of the revered late US secretary of state, had accosted the housekeeper when she came to clean his $3,000-a-night room at the Sofitel and, against her will, forced her to engage in "a hurried sexual encounter." The woman, a 32-year-old Guinean refugee, was reported to have been stunned and scared when reporting the incident to her hotel superiors. Vance's office decided immediately that the woman's story was enough to retrieve Strauss-Kahn from his plane and take him into custody.

Strauss-Kahn was thereupon hauled into court and forced to undergo the most humiliating of American jurisprudence customs, the "perp walk," wherein a handcuffed celebrity defendant is made to parade in full view of news cameras. Photos of the accused IMF head immediately ricocheted around the world, causing instant indignation in France at the "barbarism" of American justice.

If anyone looked not only guilty but at the end of his tether, it was the disgraced, imperious financial potentate, brought down by a poor, defenseless chambermaid.

A REPUTATION FOR WOMANIZING AND LOUTISH BEHAVIOR

In the chaotic days that followed Dominique Strauss-Kahn's arrest, the IMF chief was subject to a nonstop tabloid recitation of a life spent as a not-so-secret lothario.

DSK, the tabloids breathlessly reported, had compiled a long history of objectionable behavior with female associates and others. Beyond a well-documented affair with a fellow IMF economist, Strauss-Kahn was accused by a British actress of acting "like a gorilla" when the two were together in Paris and behaving like a "rutting chimpanzee" with his second wife's godchild, French journalist Tristane Banon, who eventually accused Strauss-Kahn of trying to rape her.

Regardless of the precise species of primate that the man known in his homeland as "the Great Seducer" most emulated, the revelations of sexual impropriety after his arrest in New York triggered a wholesale attack on his reputation. Strauss-Kahn quickly resigned his post at the IMF and, with it, any immediate chance to campaign for president of France.

In New York, his accuser's story was found to be "compelling and unwavering," according to news reports. Her lurid testimony included "powerful details" that were corroborated by medical examination. With a gruesome trial and possible jail term staring him in the face, Dominique Strauss-Kahn could tend to repairing his life later. For the moment, his singular focus had to remain on only one thing: freeing himself from the charges of sexual assault.

And so, he went low.

DSK PUBLIC RELATIONS STRATEGY: DESTROY THE ACCUSER

Strauss-Kahn's first decision as an accused sex offender was to retain one of New York's most media- and court-savvy criminal defense attorneys, Benjamin Brafman. Brafman had defended, among others, hip-hop music moguls Sean "P Diddy" Combs on illegal gun and bribery charges and Jay-Z on assault charges. Brafman was a student of the media who left no public fingerprints.

In entering a plea of not guilty, Brafman told the court that the evidence "will not be consistent with a forcible encounter." The attorney and his client had nothing more to say—at least not for the record.

But in the ensuing days, after Strauss-Kahn's arrest and the anonymous woman's declaration that she had been forcibly assaulted, DSK's accuser was confronted with a withering wave of anonymous reports that questioned her credibility, her veracity, her morality and her motives.

In rapid succession, over the course of several weeks, the story of Strauss-Kahn's accuser began to unravel as tabloid headlines turned against her.

- Although she claimed to have been gang raped by soldiers in her native Guinea, she later admitted fabricating the story to help her gain entry to the United States.
- While the woman insisted she wasn't interested in making money from the case, she was caught on tape discussing just that with her fiancé, a detainee in an Arizona immigration jail.

- She failed to disclose her ownership of a bank account in which other people had deposited $60,000 and from which she had paid a person she thought was her fiancé's partner in a clothing business.

The case had not yet come to trial, but Brafman and partners were aggressively pressing their case through what is known as litigation public relations. While it is often used to indirectly influence prospective jurors, Brafman was using litigation PR to pressure the DA.

As the attacks on her character and motive gained momentum, the woman, Nafissatou Diallo, shed her cloak of anonymity and went public, tearfully telling ABC's Robin Roberts, "God is my witness I'm telling the truth. From my heart. God knows that."

But if God was convinced, Strauss-Kahn's attorneys weren't so sure. Immediately after Diallo's sympathetic interviews, Strauss-Kahn's lawyers accused her attorneys of having "orchestrated an unprecedented number of media events and rallies to bring pressure on the prosecutors in this case after she had to admit her extraordinary efforts to mislead them." Diallo's broken silence, they claimed, was meant to "inflame public opinion against a defendant in a pending criminal case."

The intensive public beat down of Diallo's credibility brought increased pressure on a beleaguered district attorney to drop the charges against Strauss-Kahn. Despite cries of "cowardice" and "weakness" from women's groups, black groups and Diallo's attorneys, three months after bringing the case public, DA Vance formally moved to dismiss the sexual assault case, due to "a pattern of untruthfulness" on the part of the accuser.

It was a crushing blow for the new district attorney and a repudiation of those around the world who leapt to the woman's defense against her high-powered adversary. But for the intended defendant, it was vindication. Strauss-Kahn, pictured regularly in the press with his supportive wife by his side, was in short order released from custody, allowed to depart from the United States, and began to remake his life in France, where prosecutors cooperated by dismissing Tristane Banon's charges that Strauss-Kahn had tried to rape her.

In his first interview on French television shortly after his return, Strauss-Kahn admitted to having "a moral failing" that he wasn't proud of. But the economist was adamant that what happened at the Sofitel was "neither violence nor constraint; no criminal act." Furthermore, asserted the freshly combative Strauss-Kahn, it wasn't at all clear whether what happened in New York was the result of "a trap or a plot" hatched by his political enemies.

While many in France were aghast at what the French press dubbed his "public relations apology," Dominique Strauss-Kahn, bloodied but unbowed, vowed to regain his reputation and live to fight another day. Meanwhile, his accuser, her job lost, her reputation shattered and her life in ruins, filed a civil suit against Strauss-Kahn for "a violent and sadistic attack," seeking unspecified damages. In a prepared statement, Strauss-Kahn's attorneys dismissed the civil suit as having no merit. "Mr. Strauss-Kahn will defend it vigorously," they said.

THE BEST DEFENSE IS . . .

In the old days—before blogs and talk radio and citizen journalists and tabloid television, when those who reported the news were more skeptical about suspicions, circumspect about conclusions and adamant about the truth—it almost always made sense for those caught in crisis to take the high road.

Today, not so much.

Dominique Strauss-Kahn may well have been telling the truth. His encounter at the Sofitel could have been a setup, a consensual sexual encounter devised by a scheming female protagonist, intent on shaking down a wealthy dupe. If so, the aggressive, go-for-the-jugular public relations campaign to denigrate his accuser may have been eminently justifiable.

But what if Nafissatou Diallo's account of what happened is closer to the truth and Strauss-Kahn was, indeed, the uninvited aggressor? Would that have been reason for Strauss-Kahn to "call off the dogs" in terms of counterattacking Diallo's credibility and acknowledge the "terrible mistake" he had made? In the context of twenty-first-century reputation management, the answer is, sadly, "no."

Strauss-Kahn's best defense was an unrelenting offense that cast his adversary as the villain and himself as the victim. Politicians politely label this practice of uncovering every scandalous, questionable, unethical or illegal bit of information to defame an opponent "opposition research." It's become de rigueur in politics, because, sadly, more often than not, it works.

Once freed from the American judicial system, Strauss-Kahn returned to France and was forced to dodge additional allegations, including that he frequented prostitutes. Nonetheless, when faced with the most overwhelming crisis of his life, Dominique Strauss-Kahn never hesitated. He examined his opponent's background, discovered her vulnerabilities and seized on them. Strauss-Kahn had chosen to take the low road, and it led him to victory.

LESSONS

1. Bad news spreads like a virus, good news a lot slower.
2. Media standards have deteriorated; yours need not.
3. Hold everyone in the organization to the same standards.
4. One has a constitutional right to a lawyer but no such right to public relations counsel.
5. Ignore public relations at your peril.

6. Sadly, taking the low road often works in the twenty-first century.
7. The high road is longer, but still better.
8. In the twenty-first century, communication is imperative to salvage reputation.
9. Stand up for what you stand for.
10. The best public relations advice is still . . . Do the right thing.

EIGHT

STICK TO THE SCRIPT

Crisis Management and Mismanagement

How BP Became "Battered Petroleum"

THE GREATEST PUBLIC RELATIONS DISASTER IN THE HISTORY OF THE oil industry began with great celebration in the South Korean winter of 1998.

Executives at Hyundai Heavy Industries in the bustling port of Ulsan were ecstatic to begin construction of the *Deepwater Horizon*, the huge rig ordered by R&B Falcon Corporation of Houston, Texas. Twenty-six months later, in February 2001, the spanking-new semi-submersible, ultra-deep-water drilling rig was delivered to Transocean Ltd., the world's largest offshore drilling company, which had acquired Falcon in 2000.

From its maiden voyage, the *Deepwater Horizon* was a well-drilling colossus, trolling the Gulf of Mexico on behalf of a number of multinational oil companies, most particularly BP plc.

BP was the world's third-largest energy company and the fourth-largest corporation in the world, employing 80,000 people and operating in 100 countries. Although BP, based in Great Britain, was the biggest company in the United Kingdom, it wanted the world to know it was a lot bigger than the British Isles. So in 2001, the company formally dropped its legal name, British Petroleum, and became BP plc, to suggest its global clout and focus.

To corporate critics, environmentalists and their ilk, BP was a particularly vulnerable target. In 1991, BP was cited as the most polluting company in the United States, based on Environmental Protection Agency toxic release data. In response, BP worked hard to distinguish itself from its generally hardnosed and standoff- ish oil industry brethren, as a responsible and concerned—and approachable—company.

- It broke with the industry in acknowledging the possible link between greenhouse gases and climate change.
- It invested heavily in sustainability and biofuels.
- And it spent millions promoting its environmentally friendly views and programs in ads and public relations sponsorships around the world.

BP recognized that its reputation mattered, and it worked assid- uously to polish that reputation, while trolling the world for black gold.

BP had used the *Deepwater Horizon* to dig other wells in the Gulf of Mexico. As rigs go, the *Deepwater Horizon* was one of the most powerful in the world, a "celebrity" legendary for its renowned oil-drilling exploits. It discovered oil in the Kaskida field in 2006. It dug the deepest oil well in the world in the Tiber field in 2009.

And on the morning of April 20, 2010, BP officials supervis- ing drilling of the 18,000-foot Macondo Prospect well, 41 miles off the Louisiana coast, joined the 140 crewmen on the *Deepwater*

Horizon's platform to celebrate the fabled rig's overall record for safety.

How tragically ironic.

Ten hours later, gas, oil and concrete from the *Deepwater Horizon* hurtled up the wellbore onto the deck, unleashing a bone-rattling explosion and a massive fireball that killed 11 workers on the platform.

Two days later, the mighty *Deepwater Horizon* sank to the bottom of the ocean floor. And the BP Corporation became embroiled in one of history's most damaging corporate public relations catastrophes, costing the company billions of dollars and proving once again the ancient Chinese aphorism: "A reputation carefully honed over hundreds of years can be destroyed in a single moment."

BLOWUP AND BLOWBACK

The BP spill in the Gulf sent off public relations shockwaves all the way to the halls of Barack Obama's White House in Washington.

After an inspired run for the presidency in which he thrashed elderly fellow Senator John McCain, Barack Obama looked to be the real deal. He was smart, personable and fiercely articulate. Sure, he had little experience running anything, but after eight years of George W. Bush and Dick Cheney, the nation and the world were in the mood for inspirational change.

What the nation got, in Obama's first years in the saddle, however, was something a bit less.

Obama's problems as president stemmed, at least in part, from the bad initial hand he had been dealt: a financial crisis of mammoth proportions, nagging unemployment hovering around 10 percent, an unpopular war in Iraq and another decade-long war in Afghanistan going nowhere but down, with Americans increasingly questioning why they were spending $4 billion a month and losing more than 1,000 young American lives.

A little more than one year into his presidency, Obama's support numbers plummeted as the administration seemed impotent in the face of the increasing array of major issues.

So the last thing Barack Obama needed in April 2010 was a major oil spill in the Gulf of Mexico.

The initial administration response to the blowup in the Gulf was tepid.

Two days after the explosion and the deaths (the same day the rig sank), White House Press Secretary Robert Gibbs said he "didn't believe" the president had reached out yet to anyone in Louisiana. In much the same way that President Bush had delegated the Hurricane Katrina catastrophe to hapless FEMA Director Mike Brown, Gibbs explained that Obama had delegated the Gulf spill detail to equally hapless Interior Secretary Ken Salazar.

In the ensuing days, as public anger rose, the Obama response morphed from one of "the Coast Guard is directing the response" . . . to one of "the president is closely monitoring the situation" . . . to one of "BP has the unique equipment to deal with the situation" . . . to one of "My job is to get this fixed. BP will pay. If its CEO worked for me, he'd be fired," which Obama offered to host Matt Lauer on NBC's *Today Show.*

By the end of May, with all hope lost for a quick resolution of the raging spill, the crisis in the Gulf was rapidly becoming a nightmare for Barack Obama. The president, who had ascended to office with such lofty potential, was now officially floundering. And so, leaning heavily on advisor Rahm Emanuel, the Darth Vader of his administration, Obama opted for the same four-word course that many others before him had found politically expedient: *Blame the oil company.*

PANIC IN THE C SUITE

Meanwhile, in the executive offices of BP, the 100-year-old energy behemoth and staple of the British economy, which had decades of experience in logically and thoughtfully handling turbulent situations, all was chaos.

The oil in the Gulf was leaking uncontrollably. The "foolproof" blowout preventer device, designed to prevent a major spill, had failed miserably. The crisis was rapidly deteriorating into a full-blown media onslaught. And nobody at BP North American headquarters in sleepy Warrenville, Illinois, or at international headquarters in London had the foggiest idea what to do.

The only thing BP knew for certain in those first days of oil spill Code Blue was that it could not become another *Exxon Valdez.*

The *Exxon Valdez,* of course, was the mother of all public relations crisis catastrophes. In March 1989 in Prince William Sound, Alaska, an Exxon tanker crashed into a reef and spilled 700,000 barrels of oil into the pristine Gulf of Valdez, soiling and killing everything in its wake.

In response, Exxon, at the time the world's largest corporation, botched every aspect of the public relations response. It offered little information. It appeared callous to the environmental disaster unfolding in Alaska. It vigorously fought off attempts to charge it for the spill. And its CEO, a dour and lugubrious petroleum engineer named Lawrence Rawl, steadfastly balked at interview requests, quickly becoming known as the world's most tone-deaf PR spokesman. When asked by *Time* magazine why he didn't visit the scene of the spill until months after the disaster, Chairman Rawl memorably replied, "I had better things to do."

So BP at least was clear that it wanted neither an Exxon-like response nor a public relations Rawl replica as its legacy in the Gulf.

In theory, the company was committed to doing the right thing. But in reality, BP wound up losing every bit as much, and maybe even more, than Exxon had.

LAUDABLE BUT DISCREDITED PR RESPONSE

Anthony Bryan "Tony" Hayward was BP's young, dynamic chief executive, who rose through the ranks from PhD geology graduate in 1982 to worldwide CEO 25 years later.

An energetic and approachable Brit, Hayward had built a reputation as an outstanding geologist, a well-rounded executive in all phases of BP operations and a responsible steward of the shareholders' investment and the public trust.

In 2006, after an explosion at a BP Texas City refinery killed 15 people, then–exploration and production chief Hayward told an internal town meeting, "We have a leadership style that is too directive and doesn't listen sufficiently well."

So when the Gulf of Mexico spill commenced in the spring of 2010, CEO Hayward was inclined to "listen" to the thousands in the Gulf whose lives had been impacted by the growing disaster. Indeed, despite the fact that BP was universally excoriated—mostly by publicity-grabbing politicians, late night comedians and blood-sniffing reporters—the performance of the company in addressing the spill and its public relations program to explain its actions were generally sound and laudable.

BP stepped up to take charge of handling the spill.

This wasn't necessarily a given. There were other deep-pocketed players involved, from Transocean, which owned the rig, to Cameron International Corporation, which had made the ill-fated blowout preventer, to Halliburton, which had advised BP on plugging the

Macondo well, to Anadarko Petroleum Corporation, which owned one-quarter of the BP well. Not surprisingly, when BP pleaded with these companies to participate in cleanup costs, each BP "partner" ducked for cover.

So BP was left holding the leaking bag and admirably accepted its fate without much objection.

> *Also without prodding, BP stepped forward to declare that it would pick up any legitimate claims associated with the Gulf spill.*

One month into the spill, 65,000 compensation claims from assorted fishermen, hotel and restaurant owners, and others had been filed, and BP had paid out $2 billion. The company also agreed, at the Obama administration's insistence, to set up a $20 billion claims fund—labeled a "shakedown" by one overzealous Republican congressman—to compensate those affected.

Whether it was strong-armed or not, no one could fault BP for not wanting to absorb the full cost of the spill. While the company's pleas for its commercial partners in the Gulf to help seemed to fall on deaf ears, BP chose to keep paying, even while privately seething over the silence of its pre-spill energy buddies.

> *Having learned from Exxon's suicidal, nondisclosure policy in the Valdez fiasco, BP grimly made itself available at the scene of the spill, so that the global media could put a daily face on the worsening environmental carnage.*

On the ground, the BP public relations strategy was to use Doug Suttles, operating head for exploration and production, as Mr. Inside to handle day-to-day cleanup operations and CEO Hayward as Mr. Outside to handle the public commentary.

This made great sense—at least on paper.

As primary spokesman, Hayward—the enthusiastic and compassionate antithesis of Exxon's morose and disinterested Rawl—was the obvious choice to become the worldwide public face of BP.

"Obvious," that is, before he opened his mouth and inserted his foot.

SPUTTERING SPOKESMAN

There is no question that CEO Hayward meant well.

But in a public relations crisis of the magnitude of the burgeoning BP spill, with the eyes of the world on your every move and the ears of the world on your every word—the difference between *meaning well* and *performing admirably* is as wide as the vast ocean into which Hayward figuratively plunged upon opening his yap.

Just as Moses seemed the ideal choice to promote the Ten Commandments (but had the good sense, as we learned in the Introduction, to allow his more loquacious brother, Aaron, to do the honors), so did CEO Hayward seem the ideal choice to serve as BP's lead spokesman. As it turned out, Hayward, too, should have found a more articulate brother.

Tony Hayward served as the face of the BP Gulf of Mexico oil spill for two excruciating months before the company mercifully replaced him at the crisis helm. It must have seemed like an eternity to poor Mr. Hayward. Due primarily to a handful of spontaneous, off-the-cuff, flippant comments—and one outrageous off-duty action—he doomed his company to public relations oblivion for time immemorial and secured his own position, right up there next to Exxon's hapless Lawrence Rawl, in the Public Relations Hall of Shame.

Here are the four fatal errors that CEO Hayward committed to earn his place in PR ignominy.

1. He predicted a speedy conclusion to the crisis.

One irrefutable rule of public relations crisis is *Never, ever, predict.*

Contemporary history is littered with the carcasses of bold predictions gone awry, to the ultimate detriment of those doing the predicting.

Barack Obama's predecessor learned this rule the hard way. In March 2003, President George W. Bush declared that "the regime of Saddam Hussein possesses weapons of mass destruction (WMDs)." Alas for W, after the overthrow of Saddam and the deaths and injuries of 5,000 coalition soldiers and thousands of Iraqis, no WMDs were ever found. Two months after the invasion, President Bush landed on the deck of the USS *Abraham Lincoln* aircraft carrier in San Diego harbor and famously declared, "Mission accomplished" in Iraq. Nearly a decade later, the United States and a shrinking number of allies were still mired in the morass of a still unstable and unpredictable nation.

The lesson: George W. Bush should never have declared or predicted anything.

As much as the press and public want to know the likely outcome and timetable, in a crisis the worst thing one can do is predict what will happen.

Tony Hayward violated this principle within days of the BP spill.

Early on, he volunteered that the environmental impact of the spill would be "very, very modest."

It made little difference that Hayward's full quote was a lot more measured: "It is impossible to say, and we will mount, as part of the aftermath, a very detailed environmental assessment, but everything we can see at the moment suggests that the overall environmental impact will be very, very modest."

Too late. The "modest impact" snippet—played in an endless loop on cable TV—was enough to set a sinking tone for Hayward and his company, right out of the box.

The fact that the Gulf spill proved to have a catastrophic impact on the economy of the region, not to mention the more than 8,000 birds, sea turtles and marine mammals that would be found injured or dead in the wake of the spill, only added to the gravity of spokesman Hayward's suicidal slip of the tongue.

2. He painted a perpetually rosy picture.

Just as you never predict in a public relations crisis, so, too, do you always attempt to *play down expectations.*

It is axiomatic in public relations that the greater one tamps down expectations, the more likely one is to look like a hero if the expectations are exceeded. Simply stated, it is better to lowball potential outcomes (i.e., anticipate the worst) than it is to get everyone's hopes up and risk having them dashed.

The simple principle is that if you steadfastly tamp down expectations, people will be relieved and amazed—and even complimentary—if results turn out to be better than you let on.

As BP's lead spokesman, CEO Hayward, obviously hoping for the best, violated this simple rule from the get-go.

One example: BP first estimated that perhaps 1,000 barrels a day would leak from the rig—making the problem seem manageable. When it quickly became obvious that the problem was eminently more significant, BP raised its estimates to 5,000 barrels a day.

A disbelieving Obama administration chartered its own panel of scientists to estimate the spill. By mid-June, the Obama panel estimated that, contrary to BP's Pollyannaish analysis, 35,000 to 60,000 barrels per day were leaking.

Another example: in late May, BP announced that it would use a so-called top kill procedure, in which heavy drilling fluid is pumped into the head of the well at the seafloor to plug the leak. Hayward decided to promote the procedure with a video explaining it and then, when it was implemented, reported that all was "going well."

Hours later, the company "paused" the procedure, and ulti-mately cut it off in failure. Again, had the company cautioned early on that the procedure wasn't guaranteed and kept expectations at bay, it wouldn't have suffered the public repudiation it did when "top kill" itself was ultimately killed.

In the end, by the time the spill was capped in mid-July, it had leaked upwards of 40,000 barrels a day, a total of approximately three million barrels since the ordeal's start. This dwarfed the less than one million barrels leaked in the *Exxon Valdez* spill.

The public relations lesson was that, had CEO Hayward down-played expectations early on and warned that a greater amount of oil might leak, the company's credibility wouldn't have suffered so dearly in light of the constantly worsening reality.

3. He whined.

Anyone who has ever been stuck in the hot glare of the media spotlight, with rabid reporters pouncing ferociously on every word, understands that one offhand slip may be enough to torpedo the most buttoned-up PR offensive.

The key for a spokesman, then, is to remember that *you are al-ways on guard because you are always on stage.*

The corollary to this PR principle is *the crisis is about others—not about you.*

Once again, CEO Hayward failed to heed simple PR advice, committing yet another fatal faux pas for himself and his company.

At the start of the spill, the CEO's empathy was clear. As Hayward put it after one unsuccessful attempt to cap the well, "I feel devas-tated . . . absolutely gutted." And there was no question that his com-passion was sincere.

But after a solid month of wall-to-wall tracking of his every move and with no end to the spill in sight, Hayward was getting to the end of his tether. On Monday morning, May 31, after another disappointing weekend of nonstop spillage, with the visibly down-cast CEO once again cornered by the worldwide media, Hayward offered few answers beyond "how sorry we are for the massive destruction that cost lives, and there's no one who wants this thing over more than I do."

And then, when he should have ended his comment right there, the BP CEO blurted out the additional seven words that would eventually compel BP's board to mercifully remove him from the lead spokesman role.

"I mean," concluded the CEO, "I'd like my life back."

Taken out of context—as it would be over and over again around the globe—Hayward's ad lib remark smacked of callous, condescending, self-centered whining, utterly devoid of any sensitivity to the 11 who died on the rig and the thousands in the Gulf whose lives had been ruined.

Unfair? Of course. Obviously, CEO Hayward felt for the people in the Gulf. Clearly, he meant to leave no such selfish impression. But as they say in the schoolyard, *tough noogies.*

The point is that in the twenty-first century, whether we like it or not, *perception* often overwhelms reality.

And Tony Hayward, by virtue of this last obtuse, tone-deaf comment, was perceived by all the world as a haughty, aristocratic, to-the-manor-born Brit who little cared about the hassles and hardships that his company had inflicted on the poor working citizens of the US Gulf.

The "get my life back" comment was the last memorable statement that the CEO would utter as the "public face" of his oil company. Shortly thereafter, BP announced that Hayward would return to London and BP Director Robert Dudley would become CEO of the company's new Gulf Coast Restoration Organization and, not coincidentally, BP's new chief spokesman for the spill.

And that should have been the last that a cringing public would hear from the embattled BP CEO.

No such luck.

As fatal as Hayward's sputtering remarks had been to BP's image, the CEO would commit one final PR coup de grâce that would forever link him to public relations ineptitude.

He achieved this distinction without even opening his mouth.

4. He went sailing.

Eager, as he disastrously noted, to get "his life back," Tony Hayward, the day after being relieved of his spokesmanship duties in the Gulf, decided to jet back overseas to watch his 52-foot yacht, *Bob,* compete in a swanky race off England's shore.

Nothing wrong with that unless, of course, you happen to be the CEO of the most scrutinized company in the world.

Predictably, as Hayward rooted for *Bob,* worldwide photographers and Internet bloggers were there to chronicle the fact that "when the going got tough, the CEO went sailing!"

Equally predictably, the juxtaposition of the BP chief executive enjoying a leisurely sail around the British coast, while the oil-stained wretches of the American Gulf Coast dealt with the devastation that BP had wrought, was the final nail in BP's public relations coffin.

BP tried to play down the Hayward yacht race. "He's spending a few hours with his family," said a BP spokesman. "I'm sure that everyone would understand that. He will be back to deal with the response. It doesn't detract from that at all."

Well, actually, it did.

And just as the Gulf spill had exceeded the *Exxon Valdez* spill in terms of oil leakage, so, too, had BP's public relations handling eclipsed Exxon's for the distinction of worst-ever crisis management.

Even when soft-spoken and apologetic BP Chairman Carl-Henric Svanberg stepped in front of White House cameras to shield his malaprop-prone CEO from further scrutiny, he, too, put his foot firmly in his mouth. After BP's first face-to-face meeting with an outraged President Obama, Svanberg told the assembled media, "I hear comments that large oil companies are greedy companies that don't care but that is not true with BP. We care about the small people."

Again predictably, all that the media picked up and replayed in a continuous loop this time was the "small people" reference, which further positioned BP as an arrogant, imperial, impervious carpetbagger.

In the end, thanks largely to the unscripted freelancing of its CEO and even its chairman, BP and its oil spill would forever be memorialized as one of the worst public relations disasters in history.

Not unexpectedly, the end for Tony Hayward came approximately three months after his company's oil well blew up in the Gulf of Mexico and one month after his yacht competed off the coast of England. On July 26, 2010, BP announced that Managing Director Bob Dudley would replace Hayward as BP CEO.

NOT YOUR MOTHER'S MEDIA

BP's and Tony Hayward's public relations problems were exacerbated because neither the company nor its leader—nor, presumably, its public relations advisors—fully understood how the media had changed by 2010.

In 1989, when the *Exxon Valdez* ran aground, there were no cell phone cameras, only one 24/7 cable TV news network (CNN), and, for all intents and purposes, no Internet. The media criticism heaped on Exxon at the time was essentially generated by mass media magazines, newspapers, and TV networks, most anchored in New York City, with limited access to the Gulf of Valdez in Alaska.

Two decades later, BP faced a dramatically different media landscape.

What BP and its advisors found out—the hard way—is that twenty-first-century reporting is not your mother's journalism.

In a catastrophic crisis like that which BP encountered, the abiding five rules in dealing with the media are as follows.

1. The "beast" must be fed.

The appetite of cable TV, talk radio and Internet bloggers is insatiable. They want "box scores"—employees fired, individuals wounded, soldiers killed, or barrels spilled. And if you don't "feed" the voracious media, your adversaries (reporters, competitors, politicians, talking heads) will be pleased to fill the vacuum.

2. Speed trumps accuracy.

With apologies to the Walters—Lippman and Cronkite—Internet "journalists" don't care so much whether they're *right* as whether they're *first*. In the old days, media powers like Reuters and Dow Jones and Associated Press and UPI and the *New York Times* and the *Washington Post* also valued healthy competition. But the premium then was on *getting it right*. In today's competitive media environment, where the quick-trigger Internet largely rules, the premium is on *breaking* the news. If it turns out to be wrong, no biggie, one can always file new copy to correct the record.

3. Identify a villain.

In twenty-first-century America, people need to be *enticed* to turn from their Facebook page or tweeting or celebrity watching to focus on a real, bone fide news story. We relish controversy, strife and sensationalism. So the best way to ensure that people will pay attention to a story is to introduce conflict. Like sex, conflict sells. And the quickest way to find conflict is to identify a real live villain—be it an adulterous golf star, greedy politician, anti-Semitic movie hero or arrogant CEO and the corporation he or she represents.

4. Herd instinct prevails.

Once a storyline has been established and ratified, it's almost impossible to derail—there is no room for nuance, and there is no time to verify questionable facts. In the age of the Internet, once the media pounce on a premise—whether true or not—it quickly morphs into a "media fact." Stated another way, if the media herd brands the Apple iPhone 4 guilty of a muffled wireless signal, it doesn't matter if, as Apple CEO Steve Jobs protested in the summer of 2010, "only five of 1,000 customers complained." Apple, whether deservedly or not, has a crisis. And the company has to act (which, as it turned out, a miffed Mr. Jobs did by offering free protective cases to enhance reception.)

5. Play to your base.

Traditional journalism depended on objectivity. The sign displayed in many newspaper newsrooms read, "If your mother tells you something, check it out!" But in the twenty-first century, the quest for objectivity has begun to fray under the pressure of providing for the 24-hour news cycle. Most responsible journalists still try to base their reporting on fair-mindedness and a quest for facts.

While journalists insist they are still fair-minded, many of the news organizations for which they toil—particularly on the national level—display sometimes subtle, sometimes blatant biases, not only on their editorial pages, but also in much of their coverage and reporting. (They all deny it.)

- The *New York Times,* the nation's foremost daily newspaper, tilts left with increasing frequency.
- So, too, does the *Washington Post,* the leading political daily in the nation.

- The *Wall Street Journal*, purchased in 2007 for $5 billion by conservative media baron Rupert Murdoch's News Corp, is the leading conservative daily paper in the United States.

As to television news, the three leading television news networks—ABC, CBS and NBC—have seen their clout diminish compared to the cable networks, whose importance has increased. Murdoch's Fox News is staunchly conservative, General Electric's MSNBC is hopelessly liberal and Time Warner's CNN doesn't know what it is.

The point for anyone in the media crosshairs is to understand these biases and govern media strategy accordingly. For example, in the summer of 2010, an Obama Department of Agriculture official was quoted out of context—by a right-wing blogger—in a way that made her appear to have delivered racist remarks. She hadn't. Fox and its conservative media brethren leapt on the remarks, causing the administration to immediately seek the woman's resignation. A day later, with the unfairly accused official smiling on set at CNN, the White House press secretary apologized. And that night, MSNBC had a field day defending the woman and the president and attacking Fox and the conservatives.

Such is the state of "objective journalism" in the twenty-first century.

A smart organization should be aware of media predilections and use them to orchestrate its responses, attempting to avoid its media "enemies" and seeking out its media "friends" in order to mitigate unfair media commentary.

OBAMA'S KATRINA

As abysmal as the oil spill was for BP, it was no picnic for the Obama administration either. In fact, Obama's public relations handling of the spill was nearly as clueless as BP's.

The public relations nadir of the Bush administration may well have been Bush's eerie nighttime "keep the faith" speech in 2005 from a spookily lit Jackson Square in New Orleans, as the people of the Gulf remained stranded from the aftereffects of Hurricane Katrina and a floundering government response.

Five years later, the Gulf oil spill turned out to be Barack Obama's Hurricane Katrina. Here's why.

He fiddled as the Gulf burned.

As noted, when the spill emerged, Obama was slow out of the gate to respond.

Just as President Bill Clinton hid behind Attorney General Janet Reno when the 1993 massacre of 100 Branch Davidians in Waco brought shame to his administration, so, too, did Obama initially hesitate to take command of the Gulf spill.

The White House pointed people to the Coast Guard and Interior Secretary Ken Salazar before recognizing that the issue was far too critical to delegate.

By the time the president realized he needed to save face by flying to the Gulf in early May and promising an "all hands on deck" response to the spill, it was too late to erase the perception abroad in the land that the president was asleep at the switch.

The point: *In a crisis, a leader needs to take charge immediately.*

He bullied the beleaguered giant.

Barack Obama arrived in Washington with a reputation for cool detachment under pressure and an ability to govern with equanimity. But in the throes of his first bone fide crisis, he quickly realized that taking the easy route of pummeling an oil giant could earn him quick public relations points.

So Obama tacitly declared BP the enemy and went after the company with a vengeance that would have made Dick Cheney envious. "As president of the United States, I will spare no effort until this spill is cleaned up," he declared in his first visit to the stricken Gulf. "BP is responsible for this leak. BP will be paying the bill," he said.

Of course, the president failed even to acknowledge the fact that BP had volunteered nearly immediately to pick up all "legitimate expenses." Nobody cared. The public wanted oil industry blood, and Obama obliged.

The president's treatment of flustered BP CEO Tony Hayward was particularly aggressive, one might even say mean-spirited. On his third trip in as many weeks to the Gulf, Obama responded to Hayward's oft-quoted curious comments by stating that if he were in charge of BP, the BP CEO "wouldn't be working for me after any of those statements."

Over the ensuing weeks, the president continued to hammer at BP while steadfastly refusing to invite the company and its embattled CEO to a face-to-face meeting. When President Obama, more than a month and a half into the spill, finally sat down with BP executives, he made a point of not being photographed with the oil company cadre and particularly avoided either appearing with or even alluding to Tony Hayward.

While in the short term, Obama's harsh treatment of BP may have satisfied the blood lust of a BP-hating nation—and particularly the Democrat's liberal base—the whole approach was unseemly and decidedly *unpresidential*.

Nobody likes a bully. And ganging up on an oil company that (1) quickly admitted its terrible mistake and (2) agreed to pay all expenses associated with that mistake, wasn't exactly the best course toward a "kinder, gentler, more bipartisan" leadership.

Indeed, in beating up on BP as he did, Barack Obama left himself open to the same criticisms of "arrogance" and "politicking" that were being directed at his corporate adversary.

He couldn't plug the leak.

Textbook crisis management advice calls for *getting it out and getting it over.*

The sooner a crisis can be put to bed, the sooner we can get back to business and make people forget what just happened. The corollary, of course, is that the longer a crisis exists, the worse for the reputation of everyone involved.

In the Gulf coast, no matter what President Obama did, he couldn't plug the leak. Day after day, as BP produced live feeds from remotely operated vehicles at the bottom of the gushing well, the public was reminded that despite all the ranting and raving and be-rating of the oil giant, the spill was still spilling, and the Obama public relations mystique suffered.

Bottom line: The failure to maintain a consistent message throughout the arduous four months of the Gulf oil spill helped bury the public image of a once proud—and, some felt, "pristine"— oil giant and helped tarnish the reputation for decisiveness and leadership of a once hopeful administration.

CONCLUSIONS

So what can we learn from BP's and President Obama's calamitous handling of the oil spill in the Gulf of Mexico?

Clearly, both the oil company and the president suffered from their public relations responses to the spill. Also clearly, given the massive impact of the oil spill on human lives and wildlife, this was an extremely bad story all the way around.

But could BP and the president have salvaged more than they did? Specifically, what could anyone have done when faced with such calamity?

The answer is equally clear and simple: *Stick to the script.*

In BP's case, its challenge was twofold: (1) to quickly take action to deal with the problem and (2) to convince the public that it was both concerned and competent to get the spill corrected.

Sadly, while the company handled the first challenge skillfully, it mishandled the second challenge stunningly. BP and its advisors allowed their chosen spokesmen, particularly CEO Hayward, to depart from what should have been an agreed-upon script.

Such a script had to be tightly constructed to make only three points:

1. BP regretted the spill and was heartsick over the deaths and pain inflicted.
2. BP took full responsibility for plugging the leak and repairing the coast.
3. That responsibility included paying for all legitimate costs.

Period.

That airtight script should have guided and constrained every BP public representative. Sadly for the company, the freelancing of its CEO and even its chairman confused the issue, so that the public retained three vastly different messages:

1. BP cavalierly downplayed the significance of the spill (e.g., that its impact would be "very, very modest").
2. BP's constantly revised estimates of the spill's impact indicated that the company was incapable of fixing the leak.
3. BP cared about itself more than it did the Gulf community that had been harmed (e.g., "I want my life back").

In failing to stick to the script, BP squandered any goodwill it might have earned from seizing the initiative at the beginning. Its failure to handle the communication challenges resulted in its being perceived as an "arrogant, tone-deaf, me-first corporate villain."

President Obama's challenge was to differentiate himself from his predecessor's bumbling handling of Hurricane Katrina and establish himself as a thoughtful, decisive, fair-minded leader.

Sadly, the only decisive element of the Obama Gulf spill handling was the president's ultimate failure.

The president's script should have been written this way:

1. The government will oversee BP's cleanup and ensure that it is done quickly and correctly.
2. The government will accept BP's pledge to pay all legitimate expenses and ensure that this is done.
3. The government will work with BP and its oil company brethren to help prevent a reccurrence of this kind of tragedy.

Such a script would have reinforced that Obama was not only a take-charge leader but also one who was, as advertised, a "fairer, more bi-partisan president." It would have differentiated him from the rabble-rousers on the left calling for BP's scalp and the apologists on the right demanding that laissez-faire capitalism be maintained. It would have enhanced the perception of an evenhanded president who was above the battle, steadily directing the crisis.

Instead, the president spent the crisis bounding from one position to another—fumbling at the start, gratuitously attacking BP as the spill progressed, and then, finally, low-keying any mention of the carnage in the Gulf as the summer of 2010 wore on.

As a consequence, as hurtful as the spill was to the reputation of the BP Company, it was also damaging to President Obama. His fumbling, flailing reaction to the BP spill positioned the president as unsteady at the helm, eager to attack an unpopular opponent, and, in the end, no different from any other politician. So much for "inspirational" leadership.

By the start of 2011, with new crises to address and as the Gulf Oil spill faded from the public eye and the long-term lawsuits and finger-pointing commenced, the incontrovertible fact remained that BP and President Obama would have lost far less in terms of reputation had they simply done the right thing and then *stuck to the script*.

LESSONS

In a crisis . . .

1. Never predict.
2. Never relax.
3. Always play down expectations.
4. The news beast must be fed.
5. Never, ever wing it.
6. Real journalists and citizen journalists are not your buddies.
7. Your crisis is about others, not you.
8. Seize the agenda.
9. Always stick to the script.
10. Always do the right thing.

NINE

THE SIN OF SPIN

Renouncing the Clinton Legacy and
Embracing the "Volcker Rule"

ON JANUARY 31, 2012, THE DAY OF THE FLORIDA REPUBLICAN PRESI-
dential primary, former Speaker of the House Newt Gingrich, having just triumphed over front-runner Mitt Romney in the South
Carolina primary, confidently proclaimed to Fox News, "We're
bringing conservatives together . . . The longer that conservatives
stay split, the harder it's going to be to stop a governor who is pro-
abortion, pro-gun control, pro-tax increase. I'm clearly the front-
runner among conservatives."

That Gingrich was trounced that day in Florida, never to return to contention for the nomination, was less important than the
fact that he was telling a bald-faced lie. Not only wasn't Gingrich
"the front-runner among conservatives," he wasn't even a *conservative*—especially in the sense that members of the libertarian Tea
Party movement or even his Republican primary adversary former
Senator Rick Santorum were *conservative*.

Technically, conservative Republicans believe firmly in as little
government as possible, a laissez-faire economy, opposition to social

policy change such as gay marriage, and a limited US role in the world. Gingrich, by contrast, had been, throughout his political career, a moderate. He was far more conciliatory and compromising than conservative Republicans in his views toward government. Indeed, his primary claim to fame as Speaker was that he managed to work with a Democratic president (Bill Clinton) and later even with a radioactive Democratic minority leader (Nancy Pelosi), supporting legislation on everything from global warming prevention to the Fairness Doctrine to relaxing penalties on illegal immigrants. Such positions—not to mention such helpmates—were anathema to rock-ribbed Republican conservatives.

So how could the undeniably middle-of-the-road Gingrich get away with billing himself to Republican voters as a *staunch conservative?* Answer: Newt Gingrich was, is, and likely will be until he hangs up his political spurs a consummate *spinner*—an individual who presents facts creatively to make a point, whether the presentation is right or wrong, honest or dishonest, fair or unfair. Stated simply, Gingrich could prevaricate, obfuscate, distort and otherwise fudge the truth in a thoroughly believable and convincing manner.

Such are the characteristics of *spin.*

HOW BURSTING BUBBA'S BUBBLE CREATED MODERN SPIN

Newt Gingrich, of course, wasn't the first modern politician to use spin to alter political reality. That ignominious honor fell to his friend and former helpmate in Washington, President William Jefferson Clinton.

Indeed, it can be argued that the pervasive modern-day practice of "spinning"—defined by the late William Safire as a "deliberate shading of news perception; attempted control of political reaction"—emerged in the wake of the Bill Clinton–Monica Lewinsky scandal of 1998.

Today, Bill Clinton is the undisputed titular head of the Democratic Party. He is an esteemed former president, benefactor to poor people throughout the world, and commands upwards of $100,000 every time he appears on a US speech podium ($200,000–$300,000 overseas, and more when he runs into an Arab sheik).

But Clinton is also the only former president known to have had a sexual encounter in the Oval Office with an intern, which, no matter how his defenders spin it, will inevitably be mentioned in the first paragraph of the 42nd president's obituary.

L'affaire Lewinsky and the other extramarital sexual escapades that bedeviled the Clinton presidency ushered in the modern practice of spin. As the accusations against Clinton multiplied—a 12-year affair with Gennifer Flowers here, a forceful White House advance to Kathleen Willey there, a sexual harassment suit in Arkansas by Paula Jones over there—so did the head-scratching rebuttals emanating from a protective cadre of corporals shielding the chief executive.

Clinton's henchmen were a veritable rogues' gallery of semantic spinners—Sidney Blumenthal, Ann Lewis, Lanny Davis, Dick Morris, Paul Begala and their fearless leader, James Carville—who tried mightily to distract a disbelieving nation and convince it that their hero wasn't guilty of the offenses he was accused of.

The facts of the Clinton scandal are now, of course, well known. But back in 1998, with a good ol' Southern boy in the White House who played the saxophone and seemed to be a pretty good president, most people trusted the chief executive when he swore to the nation that, "I did not have sexual relations with that woman, Miss Lewinsky." Few believed that a man who held the highest office in the land could, in fact, have committed such an inexcusable act, much less inside the White House itself, not to mention lie outright about it. In fact, he did, it was, and he did.

Whether Clinton's lieutenants knew the truth or not didn't much matter; they initiated a round-the-clock media offensive to suggest that the women with whom Clinton was alleged to have cavorted were nothing more than—in the famous phrase Carville directed at Paula Jones—"trailer park trash."

The Clinton defense team also worked nonstop to denigrate Kenneth Starr, the independent counsel appointed by Congress initially to look into the suicide death of deputy White House counsel Vince Foster and later into the Lewinsky case. Carville and friends were adamant that the Starr inquisition was politically motivated. "Drag a hundred-dollar bill through a trailer park," seethed Carville, "you never know what you'll find. It's all about money, plain and simple, and a healthy dose of right-wing politics." And the so-called Ragin' Cajun was even more certain about Starr's motives. "There's this concerted effort to, quote, get the president," Carville said on *Meet the Press.*

Carville called the investigation "scuzzy," and his junior partner Begala railed that the president's relationship with Lewinsky wasn't what "I would consider improper." (Begala never did clarify what kind of relationship he considered "proper.")

The point is that all of these musings by Carville, Begala and the rest, which dominated the news for the better part of 1998, were nothing more than textbook spin—a concerted campaign to deflect and distract from President Clinton's horrible judgment, indefensible behavior and legacy-crippling mistake.

At the time, though, all that furious spinning worked. Clinton's approval ratings remained high throughout 1998, despite the darkening clouds converging around him. In December of that year, Clinton's job approval stood at 73 percent, with polls indicating that a majority of Americans were more upset with Republicans going after him than they were with the president's inappropriate conduct, not to mention lying.

Clinton finally fessed up about his sexual affair with Lewinsky in August 1998, after seven tortuous months of vociferous denial. After assuring the Starr panel that he would "answer each question as accurately and fully as I can," Clinton proceeded to spin the Lewinsky relationship with an artfulness that must have been the envy of even his subordinates. Proving that the tree did not fall far from the apples, the president explained:

"When I was alone with Ms. Lewinsky on certain occasions in early 1996 and once in early 1997, I engaged in conduct that was wrong. These encounters did not consist of sexual intercourse. They did not constitute sexual relations as I understood that term to be defined at my January 17, 1998, deposition. But they did involve inappropriate intimate contact. These inappropriate encounters ended, at my insistence, in early 1997. I also had occasional telephone conversations with Ms. Lewinsky that included inappropriate sexual banter. I regret that what began as a friendship came to include this conduct and I take full responsibility for my actions."

And when Starr's team questioned Clinton on his attorney's claim that there "is absolutely no sex of any kind in any manner, shape, or form" between Clinton and Lewinsky, the president famously responded, "It depends on what the meaning of the word 'is' is."

Thus was born the modern practice of spin.

And if you think that openly deceiving the public as Clinton and his advisors did would result in universal rebuke, you would be mistaken. Clinton himself remains the patron saint and go-to statesman of the Democratic Party, with a multimillion-dollar personal fortune acquired post-Lewinsky. Carville, who upon being confronted with the truth about his boss dismissed it simply as an older man "acting foolish with a young woman," is a beloved and highly compensated Democratic consultant. Begala is a CNN commentator, and Davis went on to renounce the very spinning he practiced so proficiently in the name of the president by authoring a book ironically titled *Truth to Tell: Tell It Early, Tell It All, Tell It Yourself.* Davis also made lots of money serving as "public relations advisor" to a variety of murderous African despots. And Dick Morris, the Clinton Democratic advertising advisor, simply took his propensity for selective spinning across the street and today toils as a Republican strategist.

So, alas, the moral of this story isn't that you can't possibly win with spin. On the contrary, the gaggle of guilt absolvers who surrounded our 42nd president have all done quite well. So the moral may well be that in a time when media heat (i.e., bluster) is a lot more ferocious than media light (i.e., fact finding), and where public gullibility is limitless, you *can* win with spin, particularly if you're high on chutzpah and low on scruples.

Furthermore, it might be argued that since the Clinton co-conspirators virtually all landed on their feet, spinning has become an accepted way of doing public relations, in politics and everywhere else the perpetrators think they can get away with duping the public.

That reality is part of the Clinton legacy.

WHY SPIN IS ANTITHETICAL TO PROFESSIONAL PUBLIC RELATIONS

Throughout the Lewinsky saga, the one Clinton advocate who should have been the president's chief spinner kept himself steadfastly above the battle. Mike McCurry, the president's well-respected press secretary, refused to be drawn personally into the Lewinsky turmoil. Rather, he reported what he knew to be factual and, unlike the Carville gang, offered little speculation.

When the White House press corps asked if he thought the president had a sexual relationship with Lewinsky, McCurry famously answered, "The president said he did not." While the Lewinsky story festered, McCurry granted a revealing interview with the *Chicago Tribune* and said:

"Maybe there'll be a simple, innocent explanation. I don't think so, because I think we would have offered that up already. I think it's going to end up being a very complicated story, as most human relationships are. And I don't think it's going to be entirely easy to explain maybe."

McCurry's caution and honesty didn't endear him to the legion of loyal spinners surrounding the president who expected undisputed fealty to their embattled leader. As a consequence, McCurry left the White House several months after his telling *Tribune* interview.

Unlike his compatriots, McCurry was an experienced public relations professional who recognized that his personal credibility with the press and the public revolved around one thing: telling the truth. Indeed, as any practitioner of public relations learns quickly, if you lie to the media once, they never believe you again. All you have as a spokesman for an individual or a company or a hospital or an issue is your credibility. Once you lose that, you've lost everything.

Mike McCurry didn't know if his boss was telling the truth, so he refused—unlike the Clinton sycophants—to risk his own reputation by assuming that the president was honorable. And that's why spin in any form should be antithetical not only to public relations professionals but to anyone concerned about building and maintaining a reputation for integrity.

Of course, public relations people are by definition advocates. They must believe in and support those for whom they work. Part of their mission is to interpret to the public the philosophy and practice of the people they work for. But the other part of that mission is to interpret back to management the attitudes and opinions and beliefs of the public. And when an action or performance is improper or inadequate, it's the responsibility of the public relations professional not to lie or obfuscate or spin, but rather to seek to *change* the action.

In other words, if you're not certain the president is telling the truth about his business with the intern, then it's your responsibility not to accept what you're told to say, but rather to try to find out the facts independently before assuring the public that all is right in the White House. The fact that the president's press secretary was frozen out of the reality of the president's situation speaks volumes about both McCurry's integrity and Clinton's guile.

Public relations people get a bad rap in this regard. In his well-reviewed book *PR! A Social History of Spin,* sociology professor Stuart Ewen raises a jaundiced eye toward a field he claims stresses "virtual factuality" in manipulating people's minds, moods and behaviors. The good professor's one-sided slam of a profession he knows little about is typical of the uninformed criticism the industry has attracted through the years. If you're a paid mouthpiece for JPMorgan Chase or Exxon or the Red Cross or Harvard or the conservative senator from Alabama or the liberal congresswoman from California or the prime minister of Italy, then you must be guilty, according to popular wisdom, of sugarcoating the truth so that your client prevails whenever possible.

As Ewen put it in an interview for Alternative Radio, "I think the history of public relations is a primarily illegitimate one. Most of it is about packaging reality to benefit powerful clients."

Critics like Ewen harbor a low regard for the public's ability to discern fiction from fact. The fact is that most of us aren't stupid—or at least not *that* stupid. And any institution or individual who perpetually stretches the truth or distorts reality eventually risks losing the public trust upon which most of us and our organizations depend.

A good public relations advocate must, of course, defend the person who signs the paycheck, but at the same time, he or she must represent the public interest fairly. Simply put, while it's essential for public relations advocates or advisors to support their clients, they must never do so at the expense of the truth. The cardinal rule of public relations is never, ever lie.

STEVE JOBS'S SPINNING SCHIZOPHRENIA

Unlike many others enlarged at death beyond what they were in life, Steve Jobs, who died in 2011, deserves all the accolades. Yes, he really was a visionary marketing genius, the greatest business leader of our time—and one of history's greatest innovators. But in one specific area of business performance, Jobs's record was much more inconsistent, debatable, even schizophrenic: the practice of public relations.

On the one hand, Jobs's mastery of product publicity and promotion stood in a class by itself—unmatched by any other business marketer. No other company or CEO in history could command the attention that Jobs and Apple did when introducing a new product. Apple product introductions—from MacBook to iPhone, from iPod to iPad—were events. Apple employees and supporters packed the hall, the crowds cheered the CEO's every word and the media took notice every time. It was brilliant public relations.

So was Jobs's handling of product crises. In the fall of 2007, when Apple reduced the price of its iPhone by $200 after only two months on the market, the loyalists who had snapped up the phone at inception screamed bloody murder. It took Steve Jobs exactly one day to admit the error of his ways, apologize in an open letter to early purchasers and announce that anyone who bought the iPhone early would receive a $100 discount on any future Apple purchase.

The founder's iPology was broadly hailed, Apple once again basked in the glow of positive publicity, and Steve Jobs, in the best spirit of positive public relations, had turned lemons into lemonade. So in terms of his *feel* for customer relations, Steve Jobs was unrivaled.

But on the other hand, the Apple king's legendary penchant for secrecy—particularly relative to his own health—resulted in an often frosty relationship with the media, frequently characterized by the kind of doublespeak, obfuscation and outright spin that would have made James Carville envious.

Under Jobs, Apple was among the most closemouthed companies, providing information on what it wanted, when it wanted, with little regard for the public's or investors' *need to know.* It was Jobs himself who famously told the world about his pancreatic cancer in a commencement address at Stanford University in 2005. In that riveting speech, the Apple founder talked frankly about facing death and how he was now "fine" as a result of surgery. And thereafter, Apple went dark in terms of its CEO's health. The company steadfastly refused to provide updates, respond to rumors or update the public on Jobs's health. Apple's view was that it was not the public's business. Investors insisted that because Steve Jobs was so critical to the company, the state of his health was material information that shareholders had to have to make intelligent decisions about buying, selling or holding Apple stock.

When pressed, Apple spun stories about Jobs's condition.

In the summer of 2008, for example, when Jobs canceled his annual MacWorld Expo keynote address and rumors circulated on the Net that he was dying, Apple leaked word that Jobs was "totally fine." In one fabled off-the-record interview with Joe Nocera of the *New York Times,* Jobs himself denied that his cancer had returned and ended his call by lovingly advising Nocera, "I think you're a slime bucket who gets most of his facts wrong."

In the winter of 2010, as the cancer that Jobs denied grew more virulent, Apple at first announced that its CEO suffered from a "hormone imbalance," and then, after skeptical journalists wouldn't go away, reluctantly corrected the record that Jobs's health problems were, in fact, "more complex" than originally reported and that the CEO would be going on leave. One TV reporter was outraged that, as he put it, "All along, sources inside Apple have reassured me that Jobs was firmly in charge, executing his responsibilities and performing his role as CEO."

Finally in the autumn of 2011, Steve Jobs acknowledged that he could no longer function as Apple CEO. Two months later he died and was properly hailed as one of history's greatest business executives. One of the only blots on that formidable record was the Apple founder's propensity to shade the truth when it served his purpose; in other words, to spin.

ADOPTING THE OTHER "VOLCKER RULE": NEVER SPIN

In an age where the term "Wall Street" evokes rancor and opprobrium across the land, one banker stands high above the battle (literally!), a revered figure free from any allegation of unscrupulousness.

Paul Volcker, all 6' 7" of him, remains the height of propriety and distinguished behavior.

As chairman of the Federal Reserve Board under Presidents Jimmy Carter and Ronald Reagan from August 1979 to August 1987, Volcker was a rock. He withstood withering attacks for valiantly pushing interest rates to unprecedented levels—the only way he knew to choke runaway inflation out of the system and lead the nation back to economic health.

Volcker, an economist by trade, distinguished himself by his bent toward integrity and truth. In later years, administrations of every political stripe sought to take advantage of Volcker's pristine reputation for candor, calling on him to lead nonpartisan efforts in the financial arena.

At the height of the nation's financial crisis in 2009, President Barack Obama appointed 82-year-old Volcker to head the President's Economic Recovery Advisory Board. Among his pronouncements, Volcker criticized the nation's leading banks, questioned their response to the crisis, and called for greater financial regulation to avoid a recurrence of the mortgage-related disaster that had nearly capsized the nation's financial system. Specifically, Volcker advocated breaking up the nation's largest banks, which had grown "too big to fail." He exhorted the president and Congress to prohibit banks from engaging in the kind of risky activities, such as proprietary trading, private equity and hedge fund investing, that had led to the crisis.

President Obama formally called for such refinements in January 2010, dubbing them collectively the "Volcker Rule." And Congress later obliged by folding the Volcker Rule into the July 2010 Dodd-Frank Wall Street Reform and Consumer Protection Act, which was passed in the aftermath of the financial crisis.

That, for Paul Volcker, was the good news. The bad news was that, like almost everything in the dysfunctional spin city of Washington, the *devil was in the details.* And the *details* surrounding the Volcker Rule weren't pretty. Specifically, during the public comment period, which stretched until February 2012, a continuous stream of banking industry lobbyists hammered at the rule, decrying its impact on potential American bank competitiveness. As a consequence, the Volcker Rule, initially designed simply to limit banks' speculative activities, had morphed into a gargantuan colossus, built from 17,000 comments, with exceptions and modifications galore; it became a mere shadow of its original form.

Throughout the months of spinning by the same financial institutions that, through lax supervision and cutting corners, had helped drive the financial system to the brink of disaster, one voice remained constant: Paul Volcker's. His comments on the process embodied the very antithesis of spin.

- On the people intent on eviscerating the rule he had envisioned, Volcker said, "When I first went to Washington, law firms didn't have buildings of 14 stories covering a whole block. That is all a reflection of the increase of lobbying, lawyers, effectiveness of money. You didn't have the same degree of Congressmen going in and out of lobbying firms."

- On the caliber of the people leading the business institutions, Volcker said, "There were certainly more people in the '50s and '60s that you looked up to with respect than now. The heads of the big banks generally tended to be conservative bankers and had an interest in public policy in a way that isn't viewed anything like the same extent now. On Wall Street, in particular, they're not of the same orientation."

- On US leadership, Volcker said, "There has been an erosion in trust. The U.S. is certainly a great country, the leader of the world. We can spend all we want on defense. But if the economy isn't doing well, and Americans don't trust their own government, you haven't got a foundation for constructive leadership. I like to think the world needs our constructive leadership, but it's dwindled."

- On President Obama's Recovery Advisory Board, which many judged a success, Volcker said, "We didn't fully understand the constraints you work under on an advisory committee in Washington these days. We weren't as effective as we should have been. Part of it is this cumbersome nature of disclosure and transparency which makes it very hard to have a lively debate."

- On his view of the widely hailed Volcker Rule, Volcker said, "It's become extremely detailed in application, which is partly the reflection, frankly, of the lobbying that takes place, of everybody looking for a loophole or a way to get around something, or a rule written so that it favors a particular thing they want to do. Regulators react by making another rule. And a very simple idea can effectively be imposed and regulated and obeyed, but it will be surrounded by a lot of excessive detail, I'm afraid."

- On what he would have done, Volcker said, "I'd write a much simpler bill. I'd love to see a four-page bill that bans proprietary trading and makes the board and chief executive responsible for compliance. And I'd have strong regulators. If the banks didn't comply with the spirit of the bill, they'd go after them."

- On the responsibility of the Federal Reserve Board to be transparent in its decisions, the former chairman said, "I think it's important that the Federal Reserve makes clear what its objectives and approaches are, and I will insist to my dying day that I didn't try to fool anybody."

And that's the real point. Trust, one of the benefits of a good reputation, begins with *not trying to fool anybody*—with telling the truth, with avoiding spin. And if an individual or an organization truly aspires to be a leader in the way that Paul Volcker has been, characterized by incorruptible integrity and unrelenting candor, no matter what the consequence, then they must be true to the other Volcker Rule—*never spin*.

CONCLUSIONS

Alas, in the twenty-first century, for every Paul Volcker who renounces spin, there is a Nancy Grace who lives by it.

Our old friend Grace, using bravado and chutzpah rather than talent or truth to climb the celebrity ladder, was at it again in the days immediately after singer Whitney Houston was found drowned in a Hollywood bathtub in 2012.

Grace, the sanctimonious screamer of the Headline News Network, appeared shortly after Houston's death on the network's parent, CNN, and stirred up a hornet's nest of condemnation by declaring, "I'd like to know who was around her, who if anyone gave her drugs—following alcohol and drugs—and who let her slip, or pushed her, underneath that water."

The fact that the LAPD had already reported that Houston's death wasn't the result of foul play or force or trauma to the body made no difference to "Nuke 'em Nancy." Nor was it surprising that Grace, known for her tactlessness and disregard of facts, would make such an inflammatory, off-the-wall remark. Her ratings, after all, depend on *buzz,* which depends on keeping herself in the public eye.

No, the real surprise was the deftness with which the publicity-seeking Grace spun her defense. As the backlash gathered momentum because her remarks were so blatantly offensive and incorrect, Nancy Grace refused either to apologize or even to acknowledge that her outrageous comments were a little bit extreme.

Her exchange with ABC legal analyst Dan Abrams on *Good Morning America* set a new standard in the annals of spin.

> **Grace:** Well, if you look at the entire sentence, I understand that some people would consider that jarring or harsh. But there is nothing delicate or nice about a murder, a death, an unexpected death, or an autopsy. And that is what autopsies are for. I know most people aren't exposed to medical examiners, autopsies, morgues, medical examiner investigations. But that's why you have an autopsy, to determine—when something looks to be not a natural death or an accidental death—was it a murder? Was it a heart attack? Was it an overdose? That's what they were looking at. That's what they had to find out.

Abrams: Yeah, but Nancy can't you just say that "ya' know what, I was wildly speculating, and I'm sorry. I shouldn't have said it. It wasn't appropriate."

Grace: That was not speculation, Dan.

Abrams: It wasn't "speculation" that she may have been "pushed under the water"?

Grace: I know that you have probably never tried a murder case or been in a morgue or attended an autopsy. But the reality is that's why you have an autopsy. That's what they were looking for. And in the same breath, I said there was no evidence of force or trauma.

Abrams: Then you went on to wildly speculate.

Grace: The reality is that an autopsy is a search for the truth. And for anyone who loved Whitney Houston, as I did, that is what medical examiners do. They look and see if it was a homicide, if it was natural causes or accident.

Abrams: But that's not the reality of this particular investigation. Nancy, did anyone associated with this particular investigation say they were looking into who pushed her under the water?

Grace: They were looking for cause of death. As a matter of fact, Dan, I'm glad you brought that up, because they mentioned in the discussion that there was no sign of force or trauma, which means they looked for force or trauma.

Abrams: Of course they did.

Grace: You're arguing with me over semantics.

Abrams: No I'm not. I'm arguing with you about going on television and making a comment that I think was rightly viewed as inappropriate. Sometimes, isn't it time to say that, "Ya' know what, I shouldn't have said that in retrospect." Instead, you're trying to defend what you said.

Grace: Well, actually, Dan, I understand where you're coming from, and it would have been true to say they are looking for cause of death. But what that means in the real world, not the ivory tower of Harvard Law

School, not just sitting there reading documents and talking about it, but the real world of an autopsy, of why her body was transported to the coroner's office, is to determine cause of death, whether it be overdose, natural causes, accident, or homicide. It is not a homicide, and I'm grateful for that. But I still want the truth.

The "truth?" The "truth?" Good God, girlfriend! That's the *last thing* you want!

Indeed, in this one brief back-and-forth between a devout spinner and an incredulous questioner, all of the sinister subtleties of spin are on graphic display—from the refusal to acknowledge error ("Look at the entire sentence") to the doubting of an interrogator's competence ("You've probably never tried a murder case") to the unctuous appeal to emotion ("Anyone who loved Whitney Houston as I did") to the final, pious appeal for "truth."

Of course, such behavior on television or anywhere else ought to be adjudged contemptible. But the sad fact is that in an age of diminishing standards and increasing celebrity, where many people are less curious and more gullible, and where the size of the megaphone and the Q factor—the measure of celebrity "appeal"—are often more important than whether one speaks truth—*spin* can win.

That's why Nancy Grace is a media star, and you're not.

LESSONS

1. Spin can win, especially in a society short on standards but . . .
2. . . . the truth shall set you free.
3. A man or woman on the make, not bothered by scruples, can spin to advantage but . . .
4. . . . an honorable man or woman will never be guilty of spin.

5. A public relations professional should never, ever spin.
6. The crisis will hurt you, but the cover-up will kill you.
7. The difference between persuasion and spin is the difference between reasoned rhetoric and manipulation.
8. Spinning is like lying: pretty soon you don't know where truth ends and obfuscation begins.
9. True character prevails over the long term.
10. The best way to keep track of what you said before is always to tell the truth.

TEN

RETHINKING REPUTATION

How the Most Unlikely Company
Went "Straight" to Change Its Image
and Recapture Credibility

BY THE END OF THE TWENTIETH CENTURY, THERE WAS NO MORE loathsome corporation on the planet than Exxon; or at least that's the way many Americans saw it.

Headquartered in New York City and run by a cadre of close-cropped, closemouthed engineers, the oil colossus dominated an industry that appeared to manufacture money, impervious to recession or the economic woes that afflicted the rest of society. Indeed, many believed that Exxon and its oil industry brethren were the *cause* of many of society's economic ills. As the cost of irreplaceable oil rose and the middle class suffered as a result, the only ones who seemed to prosper were the energy companies.

As the price of gas at the pump continued to increase, so did American hostility toward the "fat cats" who manufactured the product. And at the top of that American chart of derision stood the most profitable, visible and easily hated company, mighty Exxon.

That Exxon was singled out for abuse wasn't surprising. Not only was it the most prominent oil company in the world, it was also the one that had suffered the most profound and public environmental disaster in history. (Never mind that the company was and is one of history's most efficiently run businesses, making a product that the world runs on, and in the process providing direct and indirect employment to hundreds of thousands of people.)

So severe was the oil spill that Exxon perpetrated, and so catastrophic was the manner in which Exxon responded to the spill, that the event set in motion perhaps the most dramatic image turnaround in the annals of corporate communication.

After being reviled as an obtuse, soulless scourge in the twentieth century, Exxon converted itself into a company recognized, if grudgingly by some, as a model corporate citizen in the twenty-first century—all that in the wake of a lone tanker that dumped thousands of barrels of oil into the pristine waters of far-off Alaska in the spring of 1989.

THE MOTHER OF ALL OIL SPILLS

The first inkling that trouble loomed at sea was an urgent call placed to Exxon's New York City corporate headquarters the morning of March 24, 1989, about an Exxon tanker running aground just outside the harbor of Valdez, Alaska.

The 987-foot bunker tanker, regrettably named the *Exxon Valdez,* was dumping barrels of gummy crude oil in the frigid, heretofore pristine waters of Prince William Sound. Complicating matters was the fact that the pilot of the huge ship, a man named Joseph Hazelwood (It's never good news for a company when the name of its tanker captain becomes a household word!), was suspected of being drunk.

While Hazelwood would later be found not to have been intoxicated at the time of the spill, the damage was done. The spill totaled 260,000 barrels—the largest spill in North American history until BP's spill in the Gulf of Mexico two decades later—affecting 1,300 square miles of water, damaging some 600 miles of coastline and killing as many as 4,000 Alaskan sea otters, not to mention countless birds, seals, whales and fish.

Ironically, in fighting the spill, Exxon did a good job (just as BP would ultimately do) in terms of operations and logistics. It immediately set up animal rescue projects, launched a major cleanup at the sound and agreed to pick up a substantial percentage of the cost of the spill. But it did poorly in public relations, making the unforgiveable mistake—as BP would also do—of downplaying the crisis in public.

It was an error that would damage the company for many years.

NO SOUL, NO STRATEGY, NO SPOKESMAN

When the spill occurred, the Gulf of Valdez wasn't the only location where Exxon was cast adrift. At its midtown New York City headquarters, Exxon's public relations response to the burgeoning crisis was equally rudderless.

For a company used to low-keying its public profile, demurring from public debate and generally confining public statements to paid advertising, the *Valdez* crisis posed an unprecedented challenge. Exxon wasn't used to sparring with the worldwide media on a daily basis. It lacked a conceptual framework for informing the public on pressing matters. Its public relations preference, like that of many large companies, was to remain off the radar screen. And until the Valdez spill, Exxon had generally been able to maintain its preferred posture of keeping its head down.

But Valdez changed all that. The magnitude of the spill compelled the company to come forward and engage in public dialogue about what was happening at Prince William Sound. Exacerbating the company's dilemma was the remoteness of the crisis; reports from Alaska were sporadic and difficult to confirm.

With little assurance of what was actually transpiring in Alaska, no plan in place to deal with the escalating crisis, no history or experience in dealing with the media onslaught and a management unfamiliar with and prone to recoil from the public spotlight, Exxon appeared clueless in dealing with the pressing questions confronting it:

- What was the nature of the spill?
- How did it happen?
- How dangerous is it to humans and wildlife?
- How rapidly will it spread?
- Will it reach mainland America? What about safeguards to prevent it?
- What is Exxon doing to stem the flow and solve the crisis?

And one more immediate question:

- Who is Exxon's chief spokesman, i.e., its "face" to the public?

The latter question, in particular, confounded Exxon's brain trust.

A "PUBLIC RELATIONS DISASTER"

Exxon's CEO was a grim-faced, straitlaced engineer named Lawrence Rawl, an archetypal "inside man" dedicated to keeping his own and his company's light under a bushel.

When confronted with the question about whether the CEO should immediately fly to Prince William Sound, Rawl's response was unwavering. As he acknowledged later, the chairman felt from the get-go that the gesture of flying to the scene of the crime would have been little more than cosmetic. "Getting me up there would have diverted our own people's attention. I couldn't help with the spill; I couldn't do anything about getting the ship off the rocks."

So the chairman stayed home, and as a result, the Exxon Corporation was pilloried for its "seeming lack of concern." As "cosmetic" as the gesture might have been, Rawl's presence at least would have underscored the CEO's commitment to fixing the problem. When he didn't show up at Valdez, it was largely interpreted by press and public alike as corroboration of the belief that the world's biggest company, even though solely responsible for an environmental catastrophe, simply didn't care. (The CEO of Carnival Cruise Lines was similarly chastised in 2011 when he, too, refused to fly to the scene of a catastrophic crash off the coast of Giglio Island in Italy that involved the ship of a Carnival subsidiary.)

The Exxon CEO's decision not to go to the scene of the spill was compounded by a corporate public relations response universally judged as "horrible."

For one thing, Exxon concentrated its media briefings in Valdez, a remote village with limited communication facilities and a four-hour time difference from New York. The news traveled so slowly from Valdez, in fact, that Exxon management itself, both in New York and elsewhere, was frequently in the dark about changing circumstances. Public statements from the company were limited and, by the time they were conveyed, often outdated or just plain wrong. The media complained vociferously that tight-lipped Exxon was purposely stonewalling.

A full ten days after the crisis erupted across the nation's front pages, Exxon placed an advertisement in 166 newspapers to reaffirm its commitment to clean up the spill. To critics, the ad seemed like too little too late, a self-serving statement that failed to address the many pointed questions raised about Exxon's conduct.

The end result for Exxon, as Chairman Rawl himself somberly acknowledged, was nothing short of a "public relations disaster."

THE DARK AGES

The impact of the Valdez spill on the Exxon Corporation was a profound one. Where others might have used the spill as a wakeup call to rethink the policy of secrecy and selective disclosure that had led to its public relations nightmare, Exxon only shrank farther into its shell.

The company's ham-handed attempts to regain public trust were met with scorn.

- An expensive, self-serving film the company produced for its annual meeting, called *Progress in Alaska,* was labeled by *USA Today* as "Exxon's worst move of the day."
- When the consultant who devised the video wrote an op-ed in the *New York Times* defending Exxon's approach in Alaska, the National Wildlife Federation responded with a blistering letter to the editor, noting that the consultant had omitted in his article that the spill had resulted in the death of more than 15,000 sea birds and numerous otters and eagles.
- Exxon added an environmental expert to its board of directors, but only after large pension fund shareholders demanded such a response.

Plus, Valdez wouldn't go away. Periodically, the media would report on developments in the settlement of the Valdez spill. In 1996, seven years after the *Exxon Valdez* ran aground, a weary Exxon announced that after paying out $2.5 billion in total costs, the corporation was closing the books on its Alaskan disaster.

Three years later, in 1999, a full decade after the spill, the company was back in court in Alaska, asking to overturn a unique law that expressly barred one particular ship—the *Exxon Valdez*—from ever again sailing into Prince William Sound.

In 2008, almost two decades after the spill, the US Supreme Court slashed the $2.5 billion punitive damages awarded by an appeals court in the case to $500 million. It was a bittersweet verdict for the company as well as for the 33,000 original claimants, 8,000 of whom had died in the 20 years of litigation.

EMBRACING AN ALIEN, OP-ED CULTURE

On November 30, 1999, Exxon, the nation's number-one oil company, consummated an $81 billion merger with Mobil Corporation, the nation's number-two oil company, to form ExxonMobil, the largest oil refiner and one of the largest publicly traded companies in the world. And, in merging with Mobil, a company known for its sharp elbows, outspokenness and aggressive public relations, Exxon began to lift the scales of public reticence and standoffishness that had characterized and condemned it for a full decade since the Valdez spill.

Public relations–wise, Mobil was as dissimilar to Exxon as liberals to conservatives. Where Exxon was quiet, Mobil was loud. Where Exxon sought a low profile, Mobil duked it out publicly with competitors. Where Exxon shunned the limelight, Mobil grabbed center stage.

Mobil Oil responded to energy shortages and skyrocketing gas prices in the mid-1970s with a public relations flurry. It sponsored a series of energy-related cartoons for newspapers; created and placed a series of editorial columns called "Observations," discussing the implications of the energy situation; channeled millions of dollars into sponsoring lofty programs such as *Masterpiece Theatre* on public television; and, most famously, sponsored a series of feisty ads on the op-ed pages of major newspapers, offering its own opinion about energy, the need to accumulate capital in society and the pivotal role of business enterprises in a capitalist economy. Mobil's op-ed ads ran every Thursday in the *New York Times* and other publications. They were hard-hitting, memorable, and pulled no punches. In the 1970s, one celebrated ad, titled "Why Do We Buy This Space?" explained Mobil's motivation behind its op-eds:

> For 12 years we've argued, cajoled, thundered, pleaded, reasoned, and poked fun. In return, we've been reviled, revered, held up as a model, and put down as a sorry example. . . . Business needs voices in the media, the same way labor unions, consumers, and other groups in the society do. Our nation functions best when economic and other concerns of the people are subjected to rigorous debate. When our messages add to the spectrum of facts and opinion available to the public, even if the decisions are contrary to our preferences, then the effort and cost are worthwhile.

Beyond the op-ed ads, when Mobil was challenged by the media, it lashed back with a vengeance. In one celebrated instance in 1984, Mobil was so infuriated by an item in the *Wall Street Journal* about the company's decision to build a Chicago office tower with a real estate firm that employed the Mobil CEO's son-in-law that the company pulled all of its advertising and "boycotted" the paper editorially. Said Mobil's legendary blood-and-guts public affairs director Herb Schmertz, "We concluded that the situation couldn't get worse. We did it for our own self-respect."

Mobil's turbocharged public relations—unprecedented for an oil company—attracted grudging admiration even from the media it frequently cast as the enemy. As *Fortune* magazine acknowledged in a major piece about Mobil's pugilistic approach to public relations, "Few organizations of any kind can rival Mobil in the artfulness and sophistication with which it presses its opinions, whether it is advocating a national energy policy, resisting congressional proposals to end vertical integration in the oil industry, or championing the cause of mass transit."

Mobil Oil's conscious decision to disavow the low-profile stance of its industry colleagues and stand up for what it stood for was summarized to *Fortune* by its feisty public affairs director, who later wrote a book, *Good-bye to the Low Profile*. Said Schmertz, "We believe in leading, not following, taking the initiative and abandoning the low-profile policy; in a word—confrontation."

To Exxon, a company more comfortable with a behind-the-scenes presence and preference, the outsized public relations reach of its new partner had to be disconcerting, if not downright scary.

As it turned out, as a result of its merger with the public relations–savvy Mobil, Exxon was literally "scared straight."

DATA-DRIVEN AWAKENING

Faced with two different philosophies on public engagement, the CEO of the new ExxonMobil, Lee Raymond, a 36-year Exxon veteran who succeeded the taciturn Rawl as Exxon chairman, saw the merger as an opportunity for the beleaguered oil company to blend the two different approaches to external engagement.

To lead the effort to reassess, reassemble and rethink Exxon's public relations strategy and face to the world, Raymond chose Ken Cohen, a thoughtful, soft-spoken member of Exxon's legal department, to become the new company's vice president for public and governmental affairs. Underscoring the importance of this mission to ExxonMobil, the function itself would report to ExxonMobil's management committee, headed by Raymond and Lou Noto, the former Mobil chairman and the new company's president. Cohen, steeped in the Exxon tradition of deliberative, methodical decision-making, understood how the company had to proceed.

In a company dominated by engineers, "the language of our company is data," Cohen said. "Management needed to see how informed publics saw us in terms of the factors that matter most to oil company reputation."

Working closely with one of his top deputies, Suzanne McCarron, Cohen set out to create a statistical model of Exxon's reputation. And they did it slowly.

"The first two years, we studied where we were," Cohen said. "We wanted to get it right, right out of the box."

In 2002, after years of study, the company had developed a proprietary research model, based on proven statistical techniques, that tracked the ephemeral quality of "reputation." At the heart of the model was the recognition that companies and industries have distinctive drivers of reputation—that is, that what drives the reputation of McDonald's or Apple is different from what drives ExxonMobil's. Before adopting a new public relations approach, the company needed to know, first, what various audiences expected of an international oil company in general and of ExxonMobil in particular.

Using a methodical, quantitative approach virtually unheard of in a "soft science" like corporate communication—where "ready, fire, aim" is often the preferred approach—ExxonMobil selected "bellwether markets" around the world and conducted focus groups among local "well-informed publics"—analysts, politicians, environmentalists, reporters, etc.—to understand what might inspire them to respect ExxonMobil. From these qualitative soundings, the company conducted quantitative surveys to measure how ExxonMobil stacked up on these specific requisites of "admired" companies.

What the team discovered by researching these well-informed publics was painful but not surprising. The bottom line: *most people didn't particularly care for Exxon.*

According to Cohen, "Valdez was a cathartic event for this company, traumatic, and it took a toll. We turned inward."

"Silence," they say, "grants the point." And thus it was with Exxon. As Cohen acknowledges, "We are 'high profile' even without opening our mouths. And because of our high profile, we need to recognize that there are circumstances that require us to engage with a broad public audience and, if we don't, we run the real risk of ceding too much ground to our critics."

Predictably, Exxon earned low marks for reputation. That wasn't unexpected. But the company was also surprised by one particular data point, representing a reputation driver they had taken great pride in. On the key industry metric of health, safety and environment, Exxon had few industry peers. The Valdez experience had helped drive the company to enforce new, more stringent safety requirements. Improving safety became an Exxon rallying cry. And the reality, in the years after Valdez, was that Exxon paced the oil industry in terms of this all-important measure.

But perception was a different story.

Fully half of the individuals ExxonMobil researched in 2002 still associated the company first and foremost with the *Exxon Valdez* spill. The public was apparently unaware of, and therefore awarded no credit to, the company's exemplary safety record since Valdez. Clearly, the company's reluctance to put its best foot forward was hurting it. The gap between the company's negative perception and positive reality—especially on health, safety and the environment—was enormous.

Said McCarron, "That was the 'aha moment' for us."

ExxonMobil's hierarchy had now seen the proof of how poorly its company was perceived. Management recognized that, for their own well-being, they had to do better, and they committed to a public relations initiative that, if successful, would help it earn, if not accolades, at least respect from a skeptical public.

SPEAKING WITH THE ENEMY

Data from its proprietary research study enabled ExxonMobil to isolate the reputational factors that were truly important to people, assess the company's special challenges in light of those factors and compose a long-term communication plan to better correlate public perception of the company with reality. To ExxonMobil, that reality was characterized by a company committed to supplying energy responsibly to meet increased demand while working on measures to reduce the environmental impact of energy use. It was clear from its research that the widespread perception about ExxonMobil, its motivations and its methods, differed considerably from that reality. And therein lay the challenge: to change perception.

To accomplish that 180-degree turn, ExxonMobil had to, first, consider the twenty-first-century environment and, second, decide conceptually how to respond to that environment.

The environment had clearly changed from the days of the *Valdez:*

1. ExxonMobil was now certainly the most prominent company in the world's energy industry.
2. The company was associated with a myriad of complex global energy issues on which it held strong views and about which it might wish to be heard.
3. In an increasingly interconnected world, it faced expanding expectations for social engagement.
4. Communicating only through traditional "corporate publics" no longer applied; the world was now composed of multiple layers of interest groups and more distinct audiences.

5. Key audiences weren't particularly "energy literate."

In response, ExxonMobil sought to present itself as (1) an honest and constructive voice in public discourse, (2) a company defined by principles and proper action and focused on solving problems and (3) a company delivering a message that was consistent, if not always appreciated.

Nearly a decade later, in 2011, CEO Rex Tillerson articulated the results of this uncompromisingly direct communication philosophy at a luncheon in Riyadh, Saudi Arabia: "Our experience at ExxonMobil shows that energy policymaking is most effective in meeting national goals when it is driven by rigorous analysis and practical realities. And at times this means we must communicate the hard truths to policymakers about the costs of ill-informed or ill-advised government interventions—in terms of weakened growth, lost jobs, unmitigated risks, and foregone revenues."

In 2002, armed with this plan and tone and backed by years of exhaustive research, ExxonMobil embarked upon its Herculean communication challenge: to take a reputation still stained by the *Valdez* and burnish it. And one of the places it started was with those who most objected to the company's role in the world, if not to its very existence.

Like Daniel entering the lion's den, ExxonMobil took its case directly to the lair of its adversaries.

The company identified "opinion leaders" around the world—environmental leaders, nongovernmental organization (NGO) officials, human rights advocates and others not especially fond of or in agreement with ExxonMobil—and arranged two-day "get-together" sessions with senior ExxonMobil managers.

These meetings—two or three per year in the United States, Europe and Asia—were conducted informally, without recordings, transcripts or agendas, and sought no agreement on key issues. Rather, ExxonMobil had but one modest objective—to begin a dialogue. One meeting staple was a review by ExxonMobil of its updated Energy Outlook, which unabashedly predicted that society in 2030 would still require oil, natural gas and coal to meet the overwhelming majority of the world's energy demand. The meetings generally marked the first time most of the participants had ever met anyone from the company. Publicity about the meetings was strictly barred; indeed, many participants didn't want it widely known that they were meeting with ExxonMobil.

Today, ExxonMobil regularly talks to the NGOs that once despised it. The company has established an External Citizenship Advisory Panel, or ECAP, composed of representatives of the NGO and the socially responsible investing (SRI) communities, which meets regularly to discuss key issues. And it publishes an annual Corporate Citizenship Report that summarizes its community engagement activities and deliberations at the ECAP. ExxonMobil executives also host regular calls with the Social Investment Research Analyst Network, a group of analysts from the SRI community, to discuss the company's activities and energy policy. And to make sure its opinion leader constituents are updated about its positions, ExxonMobil issues a periodic IConnect email blast that provides NGO, SRI and government representatives with an early alert on developments and issues that the company believes important.

From a standing start a decade ago, the ExxonMobil effort to communicate candidly with opinion leaders has not only changed their views of the company—that is, the ExxonMobil reputation—it has actually changed the company.

Said public affairs manager Tony Cudmore, "What we say may not always be popular to all audiences, but we made a real effort to talk about the issues in an open and constructive manner."

BECOMING MORE "SOCIAL"

ExxonMobil's "engagement" with the public has, in a word, become more "social."

According to Cudmore, "No question that Valdez was used against us. As a consequence, at the time of the merger, we were clearly 'reactive,' particularly with the media."

To change its relationship with a generally hostile, unfriendly press after the merger, ExxonMobil began to build relationships with energy beat reporters and help introduce management to them. From a guarded, reactive posture, the company moved to a more open philosophy in explaining its story to the public through the press.

Suzanne McCarron described that philosophy as one of "straight talk, where we tell the whole story, not just the positives." Indeed, said McCarron, over the years, "straight talk"—speaking candidly and letting the chips fall where they may—has become the essence of ExxonMobil's corporate communication DNA.

Nonetheless, ExxonMobil decided to drop—or at least pare back substantially—the very public relations anchor that helped stamp the identity of its feisty Mobil predecessor: the weekly op-ed ads throughout the nation. They were bold and brash and uncompromising, discussing the importance of energy and oil and, heaven forfend, even *profits!* Mobil's philosophy seemed to be that if the media, in its news columns, wouldn't present Big Oil's perspective, then the company would pay for it with advertising, done in the form of opinion editorials.

By 2010, however, ExxonMobil's research indicated that readership of the op-ed ads was dwindling as individuals increasingly sought out alternative sources, principally the Internet and cable news, to find out what was going on in the world. Consequently, the op-ed ads were losing their relevance. Or, as Tony Cudmore put it,

"Buying static space in the *New York Times* print edition no longer met our policy communications objectives."

Thus was born "son of op-ed," the oil industry's first blog, published several times a week. Specifically, ExxonMobil's communication brain trust decided that the company would produce a blog called *Exxon Mobil Perspectives* and bylined by Public and Government Affairs Vice President Cohen, discussing in a clear and unadorned way periodic matters of importance to ExxonMobil and its industry, and aimed exclusively at the 100 or so most influential Capitol Hill staffers, reporters and similar energy industry watchers. Unlike the earlier op-ed, the Exxon blog allows—even encourages—direct feedback from readers.

According to Cudmore, the idea of a blog appealed to ExxonMobil on several levels. First, it offered a more flexible format than the op-eds; i.e., the company wasn't obligated to produce copy on a structured schedule, but rather as the information warranted. Second, it could be produced quickly, thus allowing ExxonMobil a rapid response mechanism for any urgent issue. Third, the blog format opened up a new form of communication with journalists, who could utilize material from the blog in writing about daily energy issues.

Two to four times a week, Cohen posts a new blog entry. In just a couple of years, the blog has posted 150 articles on major energy and corporate citizenship topics and received upwards of 1,200 reader comments. Few energy-related subjects are off-limits. According to Cohen, "The blog represents the company's philosophy of being transparent through delivering straight talk on all relevant issues in the energy space." And those "issues" run the gamut. For example:

- When the Environmental Protection Agency set quotas in 2012, requiring the nation's refiners to add 8.65 million gallons of cellulosic ethanol to America's fuel supplies, the blog dissected why the mandate was impossible to attain and, therefore, a mistake.

- When ExxonMobil announced earnings of $10.3 billion— for the quarter!—at the end of 2011, and critics gasped at the wealth in the midst of worldwide recession, the blog meticulously explained how the company's operations and investments contributed to the economy in order to generate those earnings.
- And when pundits predicted the likelihood that oil, as an energy source, would be extinct in a matter of decades, the blog studiously quoted ExxonMobil's updated Outlook for Energy that talked about a 2040 environment where fuels will be cleaner, energy demand will decline and the vast majority of the world's energy will still emanate from the traditional sources of oil, coal and natural gas.

And what about top management approval? The answer to that question is most unexpected to doubters who consider ExxonMobil a company with a backward, head-in-the-sand, low-profile public relations attitude.

"Senior management has confidence in our process and our approach," said Cohen, "and gave us the 'go ahead' to start up the blog."

This fact alone is proof of how much ExxonMobil has matured as a communicator and grown as a public citizen since the dark days of Valdez.

The ExxonMobil blog is complemented by a company YouTube site that features primarily corporate advertising and a corporate Twitter account, @exxonmobil.

At least one group of influential ExxonMobil opinion leaders has voiced appreciation for the company's forays into social media. According to Cohen, "Our employees tell us they feel good that their company is responsive and active in the public dialogue."

A NEW SPILL, A NEW APPROACH

If anyone doubted the existence of a reborn, more public relations–conscious ExxonMobil, all they needed to do was compare how the old Exxon handled the Valdez spill of 1989 with how the new ExxonMobil handled the Montana spill of 2011.

In the summer of 2011, when most Americans were preparing for the approaching July 4 holiday weekend, the executives of ExxonMobil were sent scrambling after reports that a company pipeline had ruptured under the Yellowstone River near Billings, Montana, and was dumping 42,000 gallons of crude oil into the waterway, prompting the evacuation of 140 people due to concerns about possible explosions and exposure to toxic fumes.

When reports spread around the nation on July 3 that ExxonMobil had suffered a significant oil spill, the news sounded eerily familiar—not only with respect to Valdez but also to the disastrous BP Gulf of Mexico spill of the year before.

But unlike the BP response in the Gulf and the earlier Exxon response to Valdez, this time the oil company didn't hesitate to jump into action to let the world know what was happening. Within hours of the first reports of the Yellowstone spill, a company public affairs representative was on the scene in Montana briefing the media on what ExxonMobil knew about the spill and what it was doing, in concert with state and federal authorities, to fix the problem and repair the damage.

Whereas, decades earlier, the company had been hesitant about owning up to the spill in Alaska, there was no such reluctance in Montana. ExxonMobil immediately dispatched its North American Regional Response Team—1,000 strong—to Montana to confront the spill. The president of ExxonMobil Pipeline Company, Gary Pruessing, took ownership of the problem and met the media. He was even joined by the president of the company's global refinery group. The company issued a preliminary statement expressing how it "deeply regrets this release and is working hard with local emergency authorities to mitigate the impacts of this release on the surrounding communities and to the environment."

Not everyone, of course, was bowled over by ExxonMobil's quick action. Indeed, in an era of instant social media criticism and unlimited online critics, ExxonMobil faced a fusillade of viral vitriol, the one kind its Valdez predecessors had been mercifully spared. One blogger from the Natural Resources Defense Council knew enough on the first day of the Montana spill to conclude that despite its claims of quick cleanup efforts, ExxonMobil had "chosen a path that allows for spills, and the environment and human health are often the losers." The media quoted local ranchers, who painfully reported, "thick, black crude stuck to all the grass, trees, lowlands." And Governor Brian Schweitzer, being a politician, let the company know in no uncertain—not to mention inelegant— terms that "The state of Montana is going to stay on this like the smell on a skunk."

"Initially, the press coverage was bad and largely inaccurate," said Cohen, "but we worked aggressively to provide the facts, and in a few days the story subsided."

To keep the public informed and combat negative coverage, ExxonMobil mobilized a full-court press of initiatives. Its executives met regularly with the colorful Montana governor and other officials, held press conferences and escorted reporters directly to the spill, set up a special website, ran explanatory ads, tweeted updates through @exxonmobil and posted on Ken Cohen's *Perspectives* blog—beginning the day after the spill—a running commentary of developments from Yellowstone.

ExxonMobil took special pains to keep the local community around the spill updated on developments. As ExxonMobil Pipeline Company President Pruessing told a congressional subcommittee several weeks after the spill, "Of paramount concern to us is the impact on local communities." The company established a community information line and sent teams door to door to visit 250 residents in the most impacted areas. It promised to respond to individual inquiries within 24 hours. And even though their community and workplace and environment had been compromised, most residents appreciated ExxonMobil's efforts to make amends.

Summarized Pruessing to Congress, "I am pleased to report that these outreach efforts have mostly received a very positive response. In fact, about 170 calls to the information line have been offers of help. This outpouring of local volunteer support is immensely helpful. It testifies to the resilience, industry and generosity of the people of Montana. We deeply appreciate their understanding and support."

Through the spill, ExxonMobil's CEO Rex Tillerson stayed out of the media fray. According to Cohen, "All of us felt that the appropriate management representation was in place, with our global head of refining and Pipeline Company president on the scene within hours after the spill." And while two decades earlier, Tillerson's predecessor, Larry Rawl, was pilloried for not immediately flying to Valdez, in 2011, the ExxonMobil CEO's absence from the Montana spill site proved a nonissue, and the decision not to insinuate him into the situation proved to be the right one.

While Exxon's cleanup effort in the Yellowstone River continued into 2012, with crews continuing to pull sections of pipeline from the river, the crisis effectively drifted from public view within weeks of the first reports of spill on July 3 and Gary Pruessing's confident appearance before Congress on July 21. In November, ExxonMobil announced that the costs to the company from the Montana spill would approximate $135 million and that 95 percent of outstanding claims had been accounted for. As the director of the Montana Department of Environmental Quality told Reuters, "Exxon, all in all, has been pretty responsive."

In two decades, the company responsible for one of history's worst environmental disasters and for its own miserable public relations response has literally come full circle.

RESTORING A REPUTATION

The true test of a corporate reputation is whether the company is perceived by its publics the same way it perceives itself. Most corporations have mission statements that are more aspirational—what the firm wants people to think it is—than they are explanations of what the company stands for today.

ExxonMobil's perceptual desire is clear. It wants people to know that it stands for oil, and that whether people believe it or not, oil is destined to remain mankind's fundamental energy source for decades to come.

As CEO Tillerson unabashedly declared to the Houston World Affairs Council in 2010, "The reality is that fossil fuels, and more particularly oil and natural gas, will continue to be the dominant source of economic energy for decades to come. As such, companies like ExxonMobil must maintain our commitment, through good times and bad, to the technology and innovative solutions to reach and deliver ever more challenging new supplies of oil and natural gas. This is something we have done for the last 125 years and will continue to do so."

At the same time, ExxonMobil wants people to understand that it believes in and stands for "health, safety and environmental concern." As Tillerson acknowledged in Houston, "The energy industry has an important role to play by investing in the research and development of integrated solutions that promote efficient use of our energy resources and increase energy supply diversity by harnessing, improving and advancing all economically viable energy sources."

Words, of course, are one thing. But proof through the affirmation of neutral third-party observers is another. And here, too, the new ExxonMobil has turned heads.

As no less a "neutral" third party than the *New York Times* declared in 2010, "Today, Exxon stands out among its peers for its obsessive attention to safety, according to analysts and industry insiders."

Indeed, the *Times* itself—which, in the days of Valdez, ran a prominent article about the world's largest energy company headlined "Exxon's Public-Relations Problem"—might be as good a barometer as any to indicate how perceptions have changed.

A vital part of Barack Obama's message in winning the White House in 2008 was his quest to overhaul the nation's energy policy and, with it, reliance on oil and gas. Candidate Obama repeatedly singled out ExxonMobil as an example of the kind of corporate greed that flows from the kind of dirty fuels that he would soon replace with clean energy.

Around the time of his election, the Obama-supporting *New York Times* visited the enemy camp of the world's mightiest oil company and, lo and behold, was graciously granted a no-holds-barred audience with CEO Tillerson himself.

Rather than breathing fire and brimstone over this latest political attack on his company's corporate birthright, the CEO was disarmingly philosophical. "Over the years," Tillerson told the *Times* reporter, "there have been many predictions that our industry was in its twilight years, only to be proven wrong. As Mark Twain said, the news of our demise has been greatly exaggerated."

A Goldman Sachs analyst who follows the company suggested to the *Times* that ExxonMobil was "the most misunderstood company in the world. For many people, the image of Exxon is the *Exxon Valdez*. But there is much more to Exxon than that. Somehow,

Exxon has persevered over the past 100 years with the best culture and management team any company could have."

CEO Tillerson harbors no illusions about the public's uncertainty—or, if you like, skepticism—about what his company is and does. "What we do is largely invisible to the public," Tillerson said, "They see the nozzle at the pump, and that's about it. They don't see the enormous level of risk that is managed very well to get that gallon of gas."

But whereas the old ExxonMobil might have just sloughed off that reality and continued to mine its oil and mind its business, the new ExxonMobil has responded differently. In the twenty-first century, for the first time in its 125 years, ExxonMobil is working at communicating its culture of discipline, patience and long-term vision to the outside world.

As Suzanne McCarron put it, "Nothing inside the company has changed, but now we're beginning to talk about what we're doing and are more engaged in the public discussion in the energy space."

It's unlikely that this new, more open philosophy will translate into regular ExxonMobil guest commentary on the nightly broadcast or cable news or annual Rex Tillerson appearances on *Meet the Press*. But it is a good bet that the openness will continue, especially since it's helping the company to finally become recognized for the values it holds dear.

As a Deutsche Bank energy analyst observed in 2010, ExxonMobil has shown "*a prescient awareness* that safety, caution and catastrophic risk avoidance would be key themes as oil companies were forced to push the envelope in the search for new oil. The fact is that Valdez pushed Exxon to the highest safety standards in the industry."

"The focus," added Public Affairs Vice President Cohen, "was always there, but now we are more ready to talk about it and engage with you."

LESSONS

1. It's never too late to rethink, refine and rebuild your reputation.
2. Research and thought must precede action and communication.
3. Don't be afraid to break bread with your adversaries.
4. Don't hide your light under a bushel.
5. The new ExxonMobil is a testament to the power of relationships . . .
6. . . . the power of publicity . . .
7. . . . the power of a new personal brand and . . .
8. . . . the power of planning.
9. In a day of omnipresent communication, letting others know who you are and what you stand for makes great good sense or, stated another way . . .
10. Public relations trumps marketing and advertising every time in the new media world.

BIBLIOGRAPHY

CHAPTER ONE: THE POWER OF RELATIONSHIPS

Susie Levitt and Katie Shea, founders of CitySlips, interview with authors, November 2, 2010, January 5, 2011, February 4, 2011, December 6, 2011, February 3, 2012.

CHAPTER TWO: THE POWER OF PUBLICITY

John Frazier, executive vice president of Quinn & Co. Public Relations, interview with authors, March 12, 2011, July 7, 2011, September 12, 2011, September 15, 2011, January 4, 2012.

Patrice Tanaka, co-chair and CCO of CRT/tanaka, interview with authors, December 4, 2011, January 19, 2012.

Shana Pereira, regional director, The Americas of Tourism Queensland, interview with the authors, November 20, 2011, January 19, 2012.

Melissa Braverman, former account supervisor at Quinn & Co, interview with authors, October 16, 2011, November 17, 2011, January 13, 2012.

CHAPTER THREE: THE POWER OF YOUR
PERSONAL OR COMPANY BRAND

P. Roy Vagelos, former chairman and CEO of Merck, interview with authors, November 18, 2011, December 16, 2011, January 6, 2012.

John Byrne, editor of *BusinessWeek*, interview with authors, January 21, 2012.

Al Alberts, email conversation with authors, January 14, 2012.

Judy Lewent, interview with authors, January 7, 2012.

Roy Vagelos and Louis Galombos, *Medicine, Science and Merck*, Cambridge University Press, Cambridge, 2004.

Milt Freudenheim, journalist for *The New York Times,* interview with authors, January 22, 2012.

CHAPTER FOUR: THE POWER OF PLANNING

T. Boone Pickens, chairman of BP Capital Management, interview with the authors, January 17, 2012, January 23, 2012.

Jay Rosser, vice president of public affairs at BP Capital Management, interview with the authors, January 17, 2012, January 23, 2012, March 5, 2012.

T. Boone Pickens, *The First Billion Is the Hardest,* Three Rivers Press, New York, 2008.

CHAPTER FIVE: THE POWER OF REPUTATION

Ray Jordan, chief communication officer of Johnson & Johnson, interview with the authors, January 26, 2012, January 28, 2012, March 2, 2012.

CHAPTER SIX: CONTROL THE AGENDA

David Kocieniewski, "Rangel Tries to Explain Back Taxes on Villa," *New York Times,* September 10, 2008.

John Edwards, interview by Bob Woodruff, *Nightline,* August 8, 2008.

Anthony Weiner, press conference, CNN, May 31, 2011.

George Mitchell, *The Mitchell Report: Report to the Commissioner of Baseball of an Independent Investigation into the Illegal Use of Steroids and Other Performance Enhancing Substances by Players in Major League Baseball,* DLA Piper US LLP, December 13, 2007.

Roger Clemens, interview with Mike Wallace, *60 Minutes,* January 6, 2008.

Mark McGwire, interview with Bob Costas, The MLB Network, January 11, 2010.

Andy Pettitte, press conference, Associated Press, February 18, 2008.

Alex Rodriguez, interview with Peter Gammons, ESPN, February 9, 2009.

"Woods to End Silence, but No Questions," Associated Press, February 18, 2010.

"Settlement Reached in Michael Vick Herpes Case," Associated Press, April 24, 2006.

Mark Maske, "Falcons' Vick Indicted In Dogfighting Case," *Washington Post,* July 18, 2007.

T.R. Reid, "Bryant: I'm Innocent," *Washington Post,* July 20, 2003.

CHAPTER SEVEN: TAKE EITHER ROAD—JUST STICK TO IT

David A. Kaplan, "Suspicions and Spies in Silicon Valley," *Newsweek,* September 17, 2006.

Faraz Davani, *HP Pretexting Scandal: Contemporary Management Issues,* August 2011, http://www.scribd.com/doc/62262162/HP-Pretexting -Scandal.

HP, "HP CEO Mark Hurd Resigns; CFO Cathie Lesjak Appointed Interim CEO; HP Announces Preliminary Results and Raises Full-year Outlook," *Financial News,* August 6, 2010.

"Hurd Scandal Pushes HP Back into the Middle of Public Crossfire," *San Jose Mercury News,* August 11, 2010.

Steve Tobak, "Oracle's Ellison: HP's Board Made Worst Mistake Since Apple Fired Jobs," CBS News, August 20, 2010.

Oracle, "Code of Ethics and Business Conduct," 2009.

Agustino Fontevecchia, "Criminal Charges Against DSK Dropped Despite 'Hurried Sexual Encounter,'" *Forbes,* August 23, 2011.

"Differing Takes on Accuser's Credibility," *New York Times,* June 30, 2011.

Nafissatou Diallo, interview with Robin Roberts, *Good Morning America,* July 25, 2011.

Greta Van Susteren, "Hotel Maid in DSK Alleged Sexual Assault to Give TV Interview," *On the Record,* July 25, 2011.

"DSK Admits to 'Moral Failing,' Denies Any Violence," CBS News, September 18, 2011.

Times Topics, "Dominique Strauss-Kahn," *New York Times,* March 27, 2012.

CHAPTER EIGHT: STICK TO THE SCRIPT

Barack Obama, interview by Matt Lauer, *Today Show,* June 8, 2010.

National Wildlife Federation, "How Does the BP Oil Spill Impact Wildlife and Habitat?" http://www.nwf.org/oil-spill/effects-on-wildlife.aspx.

Tony Hayward, interview by Jeffrey Kofman, *Nightline,* May 24, 2010.

"BP Chief Predicts 'Very Modest' Oil Spill Impact," *Sky News,* May 18, 2010.

Tony Hayward, press conference, *Huffington Post,* June 1, 2010.

Benjamin Snyder, "Tony Hayward's Greatest Hits," *CNN Money,* June 10, 2010.

Raphael Satter, "As Oil Spews in Gulf, BP Chief at UK Yacht Race," *The Guardian,* June 19, 2010.

Richard Adams, "Gulf oil spill: Obama and BP caring for the 'small people,'" *The Guardian,* June 16, 2010.

CHAPTER NINE: THE SIN OF SPIN

Newt Gingrich, interview by Gretchen Carlson, *Fox and Friends*, January 31, 2012.

James Carville, interview by Tim Russert, *Meet the Press*, January 25, 1998.

Starr Commission, *The Starr Report: The Official Report of the Independent Counsel's Investigation of the President*, Prima Lifestyles, September 14, 1998.

Roger Simon, "Telling the Truth Slowly: Press Secretary Recounts Strategy," *Chicago Tribune*, February 17, 1998.

Stuart Ewen, *PR! A Social History of Spin*, Basic Books, November 1996.

Joe Nocera, "Apple's Culture of Secrecy," *New York Times*, July 26, 2008.

Nancy Grace, *CNN Newsroom*, February 13, 2012.

Nancy Grace and Dan Abrams, interview by Robin Roberts, *Good Morning America*, February 16, 2012.

William Safire, *Political Dictionary*, Oxford University Press, New York, 2008.

CHAPTER TEN: RETHINKING REPUTATION

John Holusha, "Exxon's Public-Relations Problem," *New York Times*, April 21, 1989.

Ken Cohen, vice president for public and governmental affairs of ExxonMobil, interview with the authors, November 14, 2011.

Suzanne McCarron, general manager of public and government affairs of ExxonMobil, interview with authors, November 14, 2011.

Tony Cudmore, corporate public affairs manager of ExxonMobil, interview with authors, November 14, 2011.

Jad Mouawad, "New Culture of Caution at Exxon after Valdez," *New York Times*, July 12, 2010.

INDEX